CONTEMPORARY CHINA INSTITUTE PUBLICATIONS

WARLORD SOLDIERS

CHINESE COMMON SOLDIERS, 1911–1937

Publications in the series are:

Party Leadership and Revolutionary Power in China (1970)
edited by John Wilson Lewis

Authority, Participation and Cultural Change in China (1973)
edited by Stuart R. Schram

Mao Tse-tung in the Scales of History (1977) *edited by Dick Wilson*

Shanghai: Revolution and Development in an Asian Metropolis (1980) *edited by Christopher Howe*

Mao Zedong and the Political Economy of the Border Region.
A Translation of Mao's *Economic and Financial Problems* (1980)
edited and translated by Andrew Watson

The Politics of Marriage in Contemporary China (1981) *by Elisabeth Croll*

Food Grain Procurement and Consumption in China (1984) *by Kenneth R. Walker*

Class and Social Stratification in Post-Revolution China (1984)
edited by James L. Watson

WARLORD SOLDIERS

CHINESE COMMON SOLDIERS, 1911–1937

Good iron does not make nails,
good men do not make soldiers

DIANA LARY

Department of History
York University, Canada

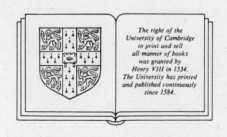

The right of the
University of Cambridge
to print and sell
all manner of books
was granted by
Henry VIII in 1534.
The University has printed
and published continuously
since 1584.

CAMBRIDGE UNIVERSITY PRESS

Cambridge
London   New York   New Rochelle
Melbourne   Sydney

Published by the Press Syndicate of the University of Cambridge
The Pitt Building, Trumpington Street, Cambridge CB2 1RP
32 East 57th Street, New York, NY 10022, USA
10 Stamford Road, Oakleigh, Melbourne 3166, Australia

First published 1985

Printed in Great Britain by
Redwood Burn Limited, Trowbridge

Library of Congress catalogue card number: 84–23803

British Library Cataloguing in Publication Data
Lary, Diana
Warlord soldiers: Chinese common soldiers,
1911–1937. – (Contemporary China Institute
publication)
1. China – History – Republic, 1912–1949
I. Title   II. Series
951.04   DS774.5

ISBN 0 521 30270 6

RB

謹以此書獻給我的導師

陳志讓教授

CONTENTS

Contents

soldier violence towards civilians – looting – rape – theft –
vandalism – the effects of violence – resistance to violence –
the self-protective mentality

ACKNOWLEDGEMENTS

Many people have helped me during the research and writing of this book. My greatest debt is to Jerome Ch'en, to whom this book is dedicated with my deep gratitude for all that he has taught me during the past two decades. Thomas and Evelyn Rawski have given me an enormous amount of help and encouragement, and the benefit of their perceptive criticism. My colleagues in Toronto, Gerald Jordan, B. M. Frolic, Margo Gewurtz, Peter Mitchell and Victor Falkenheims have all made different contributions. Other scholars in the China field have given me the benefit of their comments: Chang Wenjin, University of Pittsburgh; Philip Huang, University of California, Los Angeles; Li Zongyi and Qi Wenxin, Chinese Academy of Social Sciences; Cai Shaoqing, University of Nanjing. Ramon Myers and his staff at the Hoover Institution, Stanford University, helped me greatly with materials. I also benefited from the use of collections in China. I thank Tang Biao and Sun Xiufu of the Second Historial Archives, Nanjing, and Ji Guilin and Zhang Kejiang of the Nanjing Library for their assistance. I received financial support for my work from the Social Science and Humanities Research Council of Canada, and from the York University Minor Research Grants Committee. Chen Tiejian of the Institute of Modern History, Chinese Academy of Social Sciences, very kindly wrote the dedication for me. Doris Rippington and York University's Secretarial Services did all the typing work, with great efficiency. Nikita, Tanya and Anna Lary did not help directly, but gave me the warmth and comfort to compensate for the lonely life of research and writing.

A soldier of the Chihlian [Zhili] army, 1926 (photo by permission of the BBC Hulton Picture Library)

INTRODUCTION

> You may not need soldiers for a hundred years,
> but you cannot be one day without them.

Confucius was the key shaper of China's tradition of the dominance of the civil over the military, the brush over the sword, and yet he recognised that soldiers were essential to a state. Their role is to protect it from external attack and to guarantee internal order. If they perform this role properly, the state is secure and at peace, and they themselves may stay quietly in the background, as a deterrent rather than an active force. If they fail in this duty, tragedy follows. In the chaotic middle decades of the nineteenth century, China's soldiers did fail the country. It was wracked by foreign invasion and by internal rebellion. Since the existing soldiers had failed so abysmally, the ailing Qing dynasty raised new armies to cope with the crises, first the Xiang and Huai Armies, and then, in the last decade and a half of the dynasty's life, the New Armies. By the end of its rule, the Qing presided over a reasonably effective fighting force.

It was too late. By 1911, when the Revolution came, the primary role of the army, defence against foreign attack, was no longer crucial. Western imperialism was running out of steam in China; its territorial aims had been achieved and the infrastructure for its economic and evangelical penetration fully established. The West was turning in on itself, preparing for the cataclysm of the First World War. After their stunning success in the Sino-Japanese War (1894–5), the Japanese no longer needed to go to war with China to pursue the industrial and commercial development of Manchuria. Now that China could defend herself, she had no external enemies who wanted to attack her. Chinese soldiers did not fight again in defence of the nation until 1932, when Japan attacked Shanghai.

With their primary role in abeyance, China's soldiers were left only with their secondary role, the preservation of internal order. This role was soon distorted and then perverted as soldiers became the major disruptors of that order. The process started, paradoxically, with the revolution that freed China from dynastic rule. The 1911 Revolution was touched off by the mutiny of New Army soldiers in Wuchang against the Qing; this mutiny set off a chain reaction which soon brought down the dynasty.[1]

The successful mutineers were engaged in a righteous uprising, in the overthrow of antiquated tyrants in the name of modern-minded republicanism. They were demonstrating at the same time how powerful soldiers had become within Chinese society, since the days when the failure of the old-style soldiers to stem foreign incursion or to preserve internal peace had forced the dynasty to create new and competent armies. The central military element in the Revolution reinforced the growing self-confidence of the military; it became more and more assertive and dominant, first under Yuan Shikai's presidency (1912–16) and then in its full, malevolent flowering after his death. The concept of military deference to a civilian order, of soldiers waiting quietly in the wings for a hundred years to defend their society against its enemies, had withered away, to be replaced by warlordism, a system in which China was fragmented into a series of satraps, each controlled by a commander answerable only to himself or to those more powerful, in a military sense, than himself. The definition of powerfulness was the size and efficiency of the army a commander controlled – its size especially. This preoccupation with size set in motion the spiralling increase in the number of Chinese soldiers. Soldiers were the fuel of warlordism, the men whose numbers made the dismal pattern of civil war and armed turbulence – the mark of the warlord period – possible and inevitable.

The actual number of soldiers cannot be stated with precision. No accurate central records were kept by the Ministry of War in Beijing. Internal army records were either non-existent or unreliable. The publicly stated numbers of individual armies were dubious, since they were designed to impress potential enemies and thus were generally inflated. It is safe to say, however, that between 1911 and 1928 China's armed forces quadrupled. The best sets of figures available differ only slightly. Ch'i Hsi-sheng gives the following figures:[2]

1916 –   500,000
1918 – 1,000,000
1924 – 1,500,000
1928 – 2,000,000.

Jerome Ch'en's figures, based on detailed provincial breakdowns (with an estimated total slightly greater than the sum of the provincial figures), are a little higher:[3]

1919 – 1,400,000
1923 – 1,620,500
1923–4 – 1,500,000
1925 – 1,450,000.

These figures, which are based mainly on Chinese sources, correspond to the estimates of foreign diplomats stationed in China: for example the estimate of the U.S. ambassador to Beijing in 1923 that China's armies contained 1,125,000 men.[4]

These estimates cover only men formally enrolled in a regular army; they do not include the substantial but unknown number of men who routinely carried arms but were not in the army. The growth of China's regular armies was paralleled by an enormous growth of men at arms. In common speech China's armed men were lumped together as soldiers-militiamen-bandits (*bingtuanfei*), members of a dismal hierarchy which descended through the following levels:

major armies	(multi-province warlord cliques, the Guomindang Central Army)
local armies	(single province or multi-county armies)
petty armies	(single county armies)
militias	(local defence forces at the county level; merchant-raised defence forces)
bandit gangs	(land-based bandit gangs; pirates)
irregular units	(temporary units raised from men normally under arms as bandits or secret society members)
mass units	(forces of armed peasants, sometimes members of secret societies, sometimes political activists)
stragglers	(individual soldiers detached from their original units)
local bullies	(village enforcers).

Only the first two (sometimes three) categories appear in the formal estimates of China's soldiers, though all the others were armed, and could become soldiers just by getting into uniform.

There was no common standard of quality amongst these armed men. There were some excellent, well-trained troops, particularly in the major armies, but they were outnumbered by inferior ones. Even in the better armies, such as the forces of Yan Xishan, the warlord of Shanxi, there was a wide range of quality, from a few high-calibre units down through mediocre garrison troops to incompetent local troops.[5] If the quality in the better units was patchy, it became progressively worse as one went down the hierarchy. The only common denominator of all these men was that they depended on weapons for their livelihood.

The number of armed men in China was not excessive if one thinks in terms of a nation at war. It never reached the proportions seen in Europe during the First World War, when mass mobilisation made military service universal. In 1916 one in ten of the French population was in the army: 4,000,000 of a population of 40,000,000.[6] In Sichuan, one of China's most heavily armed provinces, only three out of a hundred men were under arms in 1932, after an incremental growth over two decades in the number of armed men. Then there were 383,500 soldiers in the province, about 1,000,000 militiamen, about 140,000 bandits, plus sundry other stragglers, thugs and mass forces (including a unit of the Red Army), out of a total population of 47,992,282.[7] The difference between France and China, though, was that China was not at war, except with herself. Almost none of China's soldiers were ready or able to defend the country. What they were able to do was to keep it in a permanent state of disruption.

In Republican China, the long process of militarisation started when the period of the great rebellions reached its fullest extent. Militarisation (*junduihua*) need not be synonymous with the growth of violence (*baolihua*); it may simply mean a rise in the status of the military, and the domination of civilian institutions by military ones, a shift, on a dipolar scale, away from the civilian towards the military end.[8] Any system that is militaristic is extremely disadvantageous to civilians. According to Alfred Vagts, a passionate critic of militarism,

4

Militarism has connoted a domination of the military man over the civilian, an undue preponderance of military demands, an emphasis on military considerations, spirit, ideals, and scales of values, in the life of states. It has meant also the imposition of heavy burdens on a people for military purposes, to the neglect of welfare and culture, and the waste of the nation's best man power in unproductive army service.[9]

Hardly a positive situation, from the civilian point of view, but still less threatening than when militarisation and the growth of violence go hand in hand, as they did in warlord China. Overt, armed power became the prime determinant of authority. The possession and use of weapons was established as the major form of power, and the indiscriminate use of violence by the trained agents of violence – the soldiers – was legitimated. Militarisation came to be inextricably bound up with the use of violence.

The violence was pervasive. On the battlefields, soldiers fought each other constantly. Leaving aside the innumerable small-scale clashes in which soldiers were involved, there was an average of eight full-scale wars per annum between 1912 and 1930. Only two years, 1914 and 1915, were free of conflict. In the worst single year, 1928, there were sixteen separate wars. Each year, an average of seven provinces was hit by war.[10] These wars caused major turbulence and disruption on their own, but the violence did not end there. Men with guns were just as likely to use them against civilians as they were against other soldiers. Chinese civilians were subjected to a capricious, arbitrary, chronic terrorism, at the hands of the 'defenders of the nation'.

The expansion of China's armies, which predicated the growth of violence, was achieved very easily; there was a constant supply of young men willing to go into the army. Enlistment was voluntary; conscription was not used seriously until the outbreak of the Anti-Japanese War in 1937. Why were so many men eager to enter a profession which had been despised in traditional Chinese culture?

As far as the military elite was concerned, the answer was that the military had become the new route to wealth and power. The army elite had ceased to be a shabby appendage to the civilian elite, as it had been in Qing society, and had become the dominant organ of society. The same did not apply to common soldiers; their social status, in terms of popular respect and of social mobility, remained low. The attractions of the army ranks were economic. Going into the army was a major new route of economic mobility, of leaving the village (*licun*). In a society made fluid by disruption, in the painful throes of political, social and economic change, four ways out (*chulu*) from rural poverty emerged: overseas emigration, movement into the cities, migration to Manchuria and enlistment into the army.

Most of the people who left the villages were poor, but poverty in itself was not a sufficient inducement to leave; if it had been, there would have been a mass exodus from rural China. For most peasants, poverty was an unquestioned fact of life, not to be relieved by migration. For others, poverty meant not only present dearth, but also lack of future prospects. For others, still, it was a relative phenomenon, in which agricultural incomes were contrasted with factory or army wages. People who held these second two perceptions of poverty were potential village-leavers. They actually left when the means to do so became available, when recruiters started operating in their localities, or transport out became easy.

The majority of leavers were single young men, without dependents.[11] They tended to come from families with more than one son, which could risk the loss of one worker for the long-range gain of remittances; families with only one son faced the risk of short-range destitution.[12] The key role of recruiters and of personal connections in turning potential migrants into actual ones made village-leaving a strongly localised affair. Almost all overseas migrants came from a few counties in Fujian and Guangdong; migrants to the cities usually came from the urban hinterland; migrants to Manchuria from specific parts of Henan and Shandong.[13] In army enlistment the geographical spread was much wider, since armies recruited all over China, but there were still specific recruitment locales, places which came to be known as 'soldier-producing areas' (*chanbing zhi qu*).

In this study I shall look at where soldiers came from, how they got into the army, what their life was like when they got there, how they were treated by their officers, how they behaved towards the world they had left, and how they were seen by that world.

There is a vast literature on warlordism in Chinese, ranging from documentary collections to detailed accounts of specific campaigns and battles to biographies of generals. Very few self-respecting warlords or Guomindang commanders allowed themselves to pass into historical limbo; they wrote autobiographies, or got other people to write biographies of them. To counter the rosy images of these kinds of books, there was a constant stream of (often scatalogical) critical books and articles about individual military figures. Outside China a minor industry has developed in warlord studies, which I have described elsewhere.[14] In all this great range of material the focus is normally on one or more of the following: officer training; army command; warlord politics; military actions; armaments; the careers of individual warlords; the role of foreign advisers; and the effects of warlordism on Chinese society. Warlord soldiers, the numerical mass of the warlord system, are left out. Only two books in English deal systematically with soldiers, in chapters of larger studies: Jerome Ch'en's *The Military–Gentry Coalition* and Ch'i Hsi-sheng's *Warlord Politics in China*. There are many studies of other categories of Chinese – peasants, workers, bandits, women, intellectuals, politicians – but not of common soldiers.[15] My intention in this study is to remove soldiers from the state of being nothing more than faceless numbers and to go beyond the blanket stereotypes, all strongly negative, which have been used to describe them in the past. There will be no attempt to sanitise them; the popular fear of soldiers was based on the real suffering and damage they inflicted on Chinese society.

Soldiers are seldom models of good behaviour, except in propaganda hyperbole. The People's Liberation Army's noble Lei Feng is celebrated because his decency and selflessness set him apart from others, and made him a suitable model for emulation. Admiration for soldiers is usually based on a dubious, macho love of fighting, not on gratitude for keeping the civilian world safe. Soldier violence pleases only the vicarious emotions of those too timid to fight themselves.[16] For most civilians soldiers are at best an unfortunate necessity and at worst a painful burden. Most Chinese of the warlord period took the second view – that soldiers were a curse. They did not ask who they were, or why they were there, they simply suffered from them. This convention has been followed in scholarship on the warlord period. My work will not correct the negative image of soldiers, since that would be impossible, but it will try to show them as products of a particular situation: as pawns in the warlord game, its victims as well as its basic material.

The study of warlord soldiers turned out to be complicated. Source materials were not obvious, and there were questions of periodisation, definition and methodology. The question of periodisation I resolved by deciding not to stay within the narrowest definition of the warlord period, 1926–8 (from the death of Yuan Shikai to the end of the Northern Expedition), but to deal with a period from the founding of the New Armies in the last decade and a half of the Qing dynasty to the beginning of conscription in 1937 at the start of the Anti-Japanese War. (I have discussed the definition of the warlord period elsewhere.[17]) The basic patterns governing the recruitment of soldiers and the norms of their behaviour were derived from the new military system introduced in the late Qing, and though standards declined in the Republic, there were few basic changes. The Guomindang set out in the mid 1920s to create a new type of army and soldier, but that effort was vitiated by internal feuding, by a growing elitism which cut the army's top off from its bottom and by an emphasis on military command and technology rather than on the quality of soldiers.

The problem of definition, of who was actually a soldier and who was simply an armed man, I resolved by dealing for most of the book with men who served in regular armies, and using one chapter to discuss the relationships between soldiers and bandits. The other categories of armed men, militiamen, irregulars and members of mass units, were all potential soldiers, but their lives were not completely restricted to the military world. I have left them on the sidelines. I do not mention, except in passing, the men of the communist armed forces, who operated under a very different military system.

The question of methodology was not straightforward or obvious. My solution was to follow the range and variety of the subject matter, the soldiers themselves, and to select a number of discrete topics, all intimately related to the life and behaviour of soldiers, and to their impact on their society. These topics were examined over ranges of time and place. I wanted to go beyond a dry recitation of facts and figures, to get a feeling for the mood of military life, and for the intangible as well as the tangible effects of soldiers on civilians. This required a topic-by-topic approach.

I did look at several other methodologies, but rejected them because they were inappropriate or because I could not find enough suitable source materials. The idea of making a composite of a 'typical soldier' was a non-starter because no such creature existed. Soldiers ranged from well-trained and well-disciplined men with superior commanders such as Feng Yuxiang, a major north-western warlord, to tattered ragamuffins serving under petty local warlords. The case study of a single region was attractive, but I could not identify a region which was both typical enough and well documented enough to satisfy me. I considered looking at a single army, but was deterred again by the questions of typicality and documentation. The best-documented armies such as the Guomindang 4th Army or Feng Yuxiang's armies were of much higher calibre than the general run. To study one of them would be to glamorise a profession which was usually sordid and brutal. The study of a single campaign was inappropriate for the same reason: the best-documented campaign, the Northern Expedition, was marked by an outpouring of idealism which, though it was soon dissipated, elevated it above other campaigns.

The warlord period was not a neat and tidy period; it was a time of chaos and rapid change. It is important in looking at it not to impose arbitrary rigidities of analysis, especially in the form of tight analytical categories, which may make an impression of reducing chaos to order, but for that reason can only be a historical falsification. I have tried in my approach to give a sense of the confusion, and at the same time of the recurring patterns within it.

As far as source materials were concerned, I had to use a variety of direct and tangential sources. There were a number of soldier biographies available, written by men who started their careers as common soldiers, but went on to make their mark in higher echelons of military or civilian life. The generals Feng Yuxiang, Luo Binghui, Liu Ruming and Cai Tingkai all started their careers at the bottom of the army. The writer Shen Congwen spent several years in the army before changing to a literary career. Most common soldiers were illiterate, however, and left no written accounts of their lives. I also looked at what officers had to say about their men. Here the available accounts created a bias towards the better units. Most commanders treated their soldiers as ciphers, in service and in the written record. Only a few commanders such as Li Zongren or Feng Yuxiang showed real interest in their men, and reflected it in their writings.

I have used fictional accounts of soldiers' life by authors who knew the army well because they had served in it. Men such as Sha Ting, Shen Congwen, Zhou Wen and Xiao Jun wrote short stories and novels about soldiers. Their accounts were marked by a compassion for soldiers and by a perception of the sad ironies of soldiers' lives and of the brutal behaviour of those who were brutally treated themselves. The fictional accounts gave a human dimension which was lacking from most of the factual ones.

There are abundant theoretical discussions of soldiers in Chinese; many of them are denunciations, as prefaces to schemes for getting rid of them, while others are explanations of the historical evolution of the military system which brought China to the point of being overrun by soldiers. Zhu Zhixin's discussions were most valuable to me, because he was not only an acute analyst, but also a patriotic revolutionary and a compassionate army commander. His early death in battle, in 1920, was a great loss to the revolutionary cause and to the Chinese military as a whole. Another very useful study was the analysis of the Chinese military system by a mysterious Russian professor of military affairs, Geliefu (Galev?), published in a Chinese translation in 1933. I have not been able to find out what Geliefu's Russian name was.

Most of the theoretical studies lack data; their authors were content to work in large, round numbers – 'several tens of thousands' (*jiwan*), or 'many' (*haoduo*). This was a characteristic of the 1910s and 1920s, when the western preoccupation with accurate numbers had still not taken hold in China. For a brief period in the 1930s western-trained social scientists did give much greater value to accurate counting and to the collection and use of statistical data. Very few of them, unfortunately, were interested in soldiers. The exception is Tao Menghe's study of a brigade in Shanxi.[18] I was able to use a number of other studies which dealt with subjects indirectly related to soldiers: studies of migration, of rural conditions and of the problems of peasant life, one of which was soldiers.

For direct observation of soldiers by outsiders, I used biographical material, contemporary journals and newspapers, and the comments of missionaries, especially those printed in the 'News from the outports' section of the *North China Herald*. These comments were usually negative, often cranky, but they were made by people who knew individual parts of China very well, and were long-term residents, able to make comparisons over time. They also wrote vivid, tart and indignant prose.

The most obvious source of information turned out to be the least fruitful – army records. Studies of soldiers in other societies have relied heavily on army records. But in China most armies kept skimpy records, which were seldom preserved. The army records which I hoped to find in the Second Historical Archives in Nanjing were not available. Published army records which do exist tend to be campaign records, lists of orders, collections of 'circular telegrams' (*tongdian*) exchanged amongst warlords, inspirational speeches and materials on military schools, all of limited use. More useful were army gazettes, the running record of activities, and army magazines, published for soldiers.

The scarcity of statistical materials was disappointing, but not an overwhelming obstacle. Very few things could be counted accurately in China during the warlord period, given the level of development of statistical services and the fact that the desire to count was not highly developed, except in commercial circles. The most reliable statistical data for the period are derived from foreign sources, and deal principally with activities in the business world. But because something is not easily counted it does not mean that it must be ignored. As David Fischer writes in his definition of the quantitative fallacy, 'there are many significant things in the world today that nobody knows how to measure ... Many ideational and emotional problems which lie at the heart of historical problems cannot be understood in quantitative terms.'[19] In other words, because a phenomenon cannot be documented statistically, it does not mean that it is irrelevant, or an unsuitable subject of study. At the other end of the spectrum, the antinomian fallacy, 'the erroneous idea that the facts which count best count least',[20] is equally dangerous. In the case of this study it is virtually irrelevant, since the problem is not what weight to give to statistical data, but simply that they are very limited.

Chinese warlord soldiers were not one of the most attractive groups to study. They had few intrinsic virtues and many vices. On a personal level, there could be no obvious empathy between a female westerner with no military training beyond the Girl Guides and the subject matter, as there normally is between women who study women or radicals who study radicals. But the influence of soldiers on the climate of Chinese society and on the direction in which it evolved was important enough to make the study worth while. Large bodies of soldiers under fragmented commands placed a great financial burden on China; they created an atmosphere of tension and insecurity which deterred economic development. They kept much of the population of China in thrall to chronic anxiety. They may not have been powerful enough to disrupt the economy completely, but

even a slightly rising income is a poor compensation for the heightened personal insecurity occasioned by political turmoil and warfare while on the contrary a low but stable per capita income may be acceptable if offered in the context of greater personal and national security.[21]

Modern Chinese society was shaped by political, ideological and economic forces from inside and outside the country; the context in which those forces worked was created in part by China's soldiers, who were responsible more than any other group for the 'heightened personal insecurity' which made revolution, a total change, a desirable alternative.

1

SOURCES OF SOLDIERS

The word 'mercenary' is pejorative; the Chinese term *guyongbing* ('wage soldier') is equally so. The words describe men who perform tasks worthy of high purpose for sordid financial gain. The mercenary fights for money, in contrast to the principled soldier (*zhuyi bing*) who fights for his nation or his political beliefs. The distinction between the two types is moral, between a base character and a lofty one. A 1938 Guomindang training manual juxtaposed the characteristics of revolutionary soldiers (*geming jun*) and ordinary ones (*pingchang jun*):

	Geming jun	*Pingchang jun*
1.	Principled	Fear death
2.	Disciplined	Undisciplined
3.	Courageous	Self-interested, self-seeking
4.	Patriotic	Money-grubbing
5.	Self-sacrificing	Careerist.[1]

This typology happens to be a Guomindang one; it could just as well have been a communist one, or one written by any patriot who deplored the inescapable fact that China's warlord soldiers *were* mercenaries.

China's situation was less unusual than the detractors of mercenaries imagined. Aside from conscripts, idealists and members of military castes, the soldiers of most nations have always been and still are mercenaries. Before the great nationalist upsurges of the Boer War and the First World War, British soldiers were mercenaries, 'odds and ends from the poorest working class, or from the Irish peasantry, enlisted for pay'.[2] Fighting for pay was not a moral problem for the men who did it, only for those who believed in higher causes, above all patriotism. The deluge of contempt which fell upon China's oblivious mercenaries came from people who were convinced that wage soldiers willing to fight for anyone who paid them were betraying China's prospects for unity and sovereignty. These critics were outraged by the mercenaries' lack of patriotism, and read it as a symptom of moral turpitude. But Zhu Zhixin, whose patriotic qualifications were impeccable, was more sanguine; he observed that 'ideology and the military are not compatible'.[3]

Zhu was not concerned with the moral character of soldiers, but with why they were soldiers at all. Denouncing a soldier as a mercenary implied that he had a choice between serving for a cause and serving for money. Zhu saw that the actual choice was one of employment, between working as a farm labourer or coolie and having a *job* in the army. A foreign commentator made the same point, in 1916:

As a carpenter is paid for making windows, so a soldier is paid for fighting battles. What he is fighting for in no way concerns him. He has no interest in the great issues at stake. He is fighting for his pay and what plunder is thrown in. He fights equally well, be his cause just or unjust, right or wrong. Should he suffer defeat he retires in no disgrace because success would bring him no glory.[4]

Soldiers enlisted with whatever unit recruited them; what happened to them after that was beyond their control. Most were straightforward mercenaries, some found themselves fighting for a cause, a principle added to their wages. The onus for transformation was on their officers. Soldiers of the Newly Created Army who became committed to revolution in the closing years of the Qing learnt their faith in the army, from their junior officers.[5] Liu Ruming, who enlisted with no thought but wages, found himself under the direct command of Feng Yuxiang, who instilled into him a sense of high cause, and of personal devotion to Feng, which lasted all his life.[6] In the Guomindang armies at the start of the Northern Expedition (1926) the inculcation of ideology was formally organised through political officers, who were able to turn mercenaries into *zhuyi bing*, and produce the courageous fighters who carried the Expedition to the Yangzi.[7]

In each of these cases, commitment to a cause was learnt in the army, not before enlistment. The idealist volunteer, enlisting to fight for a cause, was a rare creature. Officers determined whether a cause was adopted or not; officers without causes led men without causes; if the officer was chiefly concerned with power and money, so were his men. The differences between mercenaries and principled soldiers lay not in their origins or characters but in the training and indoctrination given to them in the army.

Volunteer enlistment (yibing) was a theoretical alternative to mercenary recruitment. But a volunteer system, where men offer themselves to serve a cause, can work only in an organised, homogenous society committed to a common goal, or in a society where sharp, clean political alternatives exist. A mass volunteer movement took place in England at the start of the First World War when the evil Hun threatened the destruction of the Race. The Red Army drew in volunteers when it came to offer a real alternative to the Guomindang. In warlord China the crisis of the nation was chronic, not acute, and the political alternatives were blurred and muddy. Any hope for volunteer enlistment was unrealistic.

This left *conscription (zhengbing)* as the only conceivable alternative to a mercenary system. Conscription often appeals to governments, because it is a quick and cheap way of getting troops, but its application is limited in that it demands either an efficient administrative system, or a willingness to press-gang. In China neither existed. And yet those who bewailed the mercenary system saw conscription as the solution, the means of ridding China of predatory soldiers – and at the same time the way to transform the status of the military within Chinese society. With conscription, China would cease to be a 'non-military culture' *(wubing de wenhua)*, in which the military was an unsavoury adjunct of civilian society; instead the military would become part of the mainstream, a new military composed of 'cultured soldiers' *(you wenhua de bing)*, the best of Chinese youth recruited by universal conscription.[8]

The advocates of conscription harked back to pre-Song China, when, they claimed, the military had stood in high repute, and soldiers had been conscripted. Conscription had fostered a sense of duty, and had kept the army tightly integrated into peasant society *(yu bing yu nong)*. With the Song introduction of mercenary enlistment, the calibre of men had fallen, until only the dregs of society went into the army.[9] Wang Anshi, the antique darling of progressive modern Chinese, was praised for his opposition to mercenary enlistment, and for his advocacy of conscription.[10] Some of the proponents of conscription were civilian reformers and politicians, others were serving officers. One of the most zealous was the Guangxi general Bai

Chongxi, whose ambition was to 'militarise' (*junduihua*) society by instituting a system of universal military training through the militia, from which men could then be conscripted for regular army service.[11]

Advocacy of conscription was a long way from implementation. Plans were drawn up periodically, but none went far. Yuan Shikai floated a scheme in 1912, and issued formal plans in 1915. Conscription was held up as the way to 'remove the stigma attaching to military service', to create an army 'animated by a national as opposed to a provincial or party spirit'.[12] The schemes died with Yuan; none of the plans of the civilian reformers got off paper. Bai Chongxi went some way with the Guangxi militia system, but never made it universal, even in his own province.[13]

The nearest thing to conscription seen in the warlord period was press-ganging, the kidnapping of men to serve in the army. Press-ganging for soldiers was rare; it was usually limited to forcing men to work as coolies for the army (*lafu*).[14] Men were seized for soldiers only when an army was desperate; and these produced men who would take the first chance to desert. In 1926 the streets of Chengdu were scoured to get men to defend the city against an impending attack,[15] and in 1933 Sichuanese peasants were press-ganged to attack the communists in the north of the province.[16] Generally forcible conscription was not used, because it produced soldiers who were useless as fighters, and had constantly to be guarded.

Not until the Anti-Japanese War did conscription become widespread. In 1936 the Nanjing government made its conscription laws operational. After that, every young male (*zhuangding*) was technically liable for military service.[17] Ironically, when the nation was in maximum danger and so patriotic volunteers might have been expected, China was visited instead by the sight of pathetic, roped conscripts being marched off to 'save the country'.[18] Conscription produced not volunteers but evaders. In Henan, practically on the front line, conscription teams found almost no volunteers in 1937; only 120 out of 224,539 eligible men volunteered.[19] In northern Jiangsu conscriptors were chased away by their prey,[20] while in west Hunan men fled into the hills and became bandits rather than be taken as soldiers.[21] Men mutilated themselves, made phoney family divisions (to establish themselves as heads of household), had themselves falsely classified as teachers, civil servants or students

16

(protected categories), even registered themselves as opium addicts – all to avoid conscription.[22] Above all they bribed their way out. Only the poor, the weak and the stupid were conscripted – or those who were paid by their communities to go. In 1942, in Henan, a man could get $2,000 to let himself be conscripted, and this huge sum was payable in a time of drought when prices were low.[23]

The failure of conscription underlined the death of idealism in Guomindang China, and of the power to inspire men to serve. Yet in the mid 1920s the Guomindang had been able to command idealism and to defeat warlordism and imperialism. By 1928 wracking internal dissension had drained away commitment to the cause. Few of the 'principled soldiers' who had struck terror into warlord hearts were still inspired. One disillusioned fighter wrote at the end of the Northern Expedition:

When we were in Guangdong, there wasn't a single man, officer or ordinary soldier, who could not utter a few knowledgeable words. But now neither the officers nor the political instructors understand principles; the soldiers, it goes without saying, are the same. As it stands now, we are gradually going back to the warlord model.[24]

Idealism still existed in some places. After 1931, the Manchurian Volunteers fought the Japanese ferociously; at their peak they numbered 40,000.[25] The Red Army drew in men committed to fighting the Japanese, fighting the Guomindang or fighting for socialism. Otherwise Zhu Zhixin's pronouncement that 'ideology and the military are not compatible' was sadly accurate.

Men were not willing to volunteer, or to serve as conscripts, but there was never a shortage of mercenaries. To understand why men went so willingly into the army as mercenaries we have to look first at what made them leave home, and then at what attracted them to the army. Poverty was the strongest pressure pushing young men out of rural society. One of Feng Yuxiang's recruits gave a succinct answer to a visiting foreigner (in 1923): 'Asked why he wished to become a soldier, one of the rustic recruits said that he had nothing to do at home, at home there was nothing to eat, but here he would get some chow.'[26] Deng Baosan enlisted at the age of fifteen because his impoverished family was no longer able to feed him.[27] The army recognised its attraction as a rice bowl; the 1938 training manual mentioned above emphasised that the army's standard of living was excellent (*shengji lianghao*).[28]

Second and subsequent sons of poor peasant families were particularly likely to see the army as an escape from poverty, for they were less crucial to the family economy than first sons. Seventy-nine per cent of the soldiers of a Taiyuan unit surveyed by Tao Menghe in 1929 were younger sons.[29] They were disadvantaged by birth and threatened with sinking further. Unemployed drifters (*wuye youmin*), already at the bottom of the economic heap, had even fewer prospects, and saw the army as their best chance of regular food, irregular pay and occasional loot, a rich contrast to rural unemployment.

Poverty alone was not a sufficient motive for enlistment. Able-bodied young men were less likely to starve than any other category of the poverty-stricken population. They could work as hired hands, migrate elsewhere, or work as coolies. Poverty had to be combined with other factors and other motives to get a young man into the army.

One motive was the search for security. Army pay was unreliable, but much less so than farm income. A soldier's wages did not depend on the weather, taxation, rent, interest payments or fluctuating prices. Men who found the chronic insecurity of farm income hard to cope with could find comparative security in the army.

The army was also an escape from the grinding toil of farm life. In contrast to the unremitting labour of farming, the army seemed to be long periods of relaxation punctuated by occasional spells of fighting. The vision of an easy life was compelling, as a plaintive comment from a missionary in Sichuan indicated: 'Labourers of every kind are hard to procure, even at increased wages. They prefer to join the ranks of soldiers who have an easy life with lots to eat and better wages.'[30] The easy life might be a mirage, but a real choice *seemed* to exist, between being poor and working like a dog, and being less poor and taking it easy. The risks of army life were greater, but so were the rewards.

Sometimes the contrast between civilian and army life was accentuated by the offer of enlistment bonuses, 'expenses to settle the family' (*anjia fei*). The amounts paid could be substantial. In Xuanwei (Yunnan) the bonus paid in 1913 was 30 *yuan*, in 1928, 80 *yuan*.[31] According to a general study of the Chinese army, bonuses were in the range of 20 to 30 *yuan*.[32] Thirty *yuan* was the amount paid in Xuchang (Henan) in 1930.[33] In many instances bonuses were not paid at all, but when they were they were a powerful incentive to enlist – a windfall to a man's family of roughly a year's wages as a labourer.

Other motives besides a desire to escape poverty played their part in enlistment. For some enlistment was an escape from boredom, an exciting alternative to the drab possibilities offered to restless young men in rural life. Qi Xieyuan was apprenticed as a clerk in a rice shop in a small town; he was so bored that when he saw a recruiting poster he enlisted on the spur of the moment.[34] Liu Ruming also found the life of an apprentice impossibly limited; he enlisted to escape it.[35]

Other recruits were escaping from more serious problems than boredom. The army was the ideal bolt-hole for young men in trouble with the law or with their families (see appendix 2). Enlistment made a man immune from prosecution, or from the assaults of his enemies. Han Fuqu was such an obstreperous youth that his family pushed him into the army, the only institution other than a prison willing to have him.[36] Armies provided a home from home for young men unhappy in their families. Cai Tingkai ran away to the army to get away from his step-mother.[37] Peng Dehuai was also forced to leave home because he was 'dissatisfied with the maltreatment of his step-mother'. He was nine when he left home, and took eight years of odd jobs before he found his true niche in the army.[38]

Whatever the motive, enlistment was the most immediate way out from rural poverty for many young men. It was not equally spread over China; some regions produced many more soldiers than others, both for local service and for export. Certain regions produced soldiers as other regions produced overseas emigrants. The soldier-producing regions (*chanbing zhi qu*) were generally poor, backward and removed from major commercial and industrial centres. Regions with easy access to cities or to abroad tended not to produce many soldiers. Being a soldier in such regions, or in any prosperous region of China, tended to come low down on the list of attractive exits from rural life.[39]

The size of soldier-producing regions varied: sometimes a whole province, sometimes a multi-*xian* region, sometimes a single *xian*. Shandong, Henan and Hebei were major producers, each province very poor, overpopulated and underdeveloped. Army service and migration to Manchuria were the only ways out. 'The phrase "good men do not become soldiers, good iron is not used for nails" is rare in the lexicon of the Henan people.'[40] The west Hunan–east Guizhou region was always an important source of soldiers, poor, backward and remote.[41] Soldiers were one of the few products of poverty-stricken Guangxi.[42]

There were regions which produced soldiers as *by-products of the endemic violence* in which they existed, armed camps where civilian rule was in abeyance, and bearing arms the norm. The Xu-Hai region of northern Jiangsu was stuck in a form of despotic feudalism. Its villages were walled enclosures (*zhai*), dominated by the mansion of the local lord (*zhaizhu*); the peasants were his tenants and armed retainers.[43] In this grim world the gun ruled; peasants working in the fields were armed, travellers carried weapons, the elite had body-guards.[44] In 1930, a local estimate put the number of guns in the region at 200,000.[45] The area produced unskilled, illiterate but very tough men; some went south of the Yangzi to work as coolies, others into professional fighting, as militiamen, bandits – or soldiers.

To the north and west of Xu-Hai lay the four-province border region of Anhui–Henan–Shandong–Jiangsu, where every village was armed, every hill-top had a fort. The region was as heavily armed as Xu-Hai. The gazetteer of Linquan (Anhui) reported in 1936 that there were 7,149 rifles in the country, 239 with the militia and 6,910 in 'private hands' (*sanbu minjian*).[46] Foreigners called the region the Badlands. It was an anarchic, turbulent place constantly at war with itself, and exporting its violence in the form of recruits to armies else-where.

In other regions *chronic local feuding* created the breeding-ground for pugnacious men whose aggression could be channelled into soldier-ing. He Long recruited this type of man in Sangzhi (Hunan), a county beset by ceaseless feuding over water rights and land bound-aries. To survive in this atmosphere of deadly animosity, a man had to be tough; tough men made good soldiers. They were willing to go into the army, but only to serve with a man they knew. He Long used his secret society connections to recruit them.

Though a wild man is a wild man, these men had their good points; they were straight-forward, they were hardy and they had character. If they didn't want to have anything to do with you they didn't, but once they came to trust you, nothing could alter their trust.[47]

The clans of Guangdong produced the same types, men who had grown up in an atmosphere of clan feuding. They made good soldiers for a commander who could direct their hostility against his own enemies. A local missionary was inspired to compare Guangdong's clansmen (and Guangxi's) with the Highland Scots:

Since the Union of Scotland and England, the military history of the United Kingdom has been enriched by many glorious pages in which the exploits of the Scottish clansmen claimed pride of place. Though the analogy between the clans of the two Kuangs and Scotland is not perfect, the successful diversion of the latter into a wider channel affords encouragement of a similar achievement in regard to the mountaineers of south China.[48]

These regions where tough men flourished in the context of established patterns of feuding were popular with recruiters, but they were not fully mercenary regions, as were Xu-Hai or the Badlands. Personal connections were essential for recruitment. Men fought for wages, but only for commanders to whom they were connected through some previous tie.

Men who had *martial arts training* or were members of martial societies were another source of skilled fighters. Regions where these activities were developed were important recruitment pools. In Kaifeng (Henan) the courtyard of the Daxiangguo Temple was usually full of young men practising martial arts, sword fighting and boxing – potential army recruits.[49] In Shaanxi there was a loose-knit society of swordsmen (*daoke*), free lances who were willing to practise their craft for anyone who would pay them.[50] In the Right and Left River Valleys of Guangxi were semi-organised braves (*youyong*), descendents of Liu Rongfu's Black Flags, who bore arms and dressed in black. They were easily recruited into regular armies. Li Zongren collected the bulk of his 7th Army from this region.[51]

Chinese recruiters ignored one source of born fighters: the ethnic minorities, rebellious, angry people. The problem was that for the minorities, all Han were enemies, to be fought against, not for. Only acculturated minorities appeared as regular soldiers, and then they served men of their own ethnic origin – the Lolo of Long Yun, the Zhuang of Lu Rongting. The one minority whose martial skills had brought it to dominance in China had forgotten how to fight. By the warlord period, the Manchu martial tradition was dead.

In addition to all these regions where some pattern of violence, feuding or martial training made military service a natural career, there were other regions in which enlistment had evolved into an *established form of employment.* Movement into the army followed a pre-scribed pattern – sons joined their fathers, friends their friends. The young men of the Guangdong Delta went abroad as a natural alternative to staying at home; their counterparts in the Nanlu region of Guangdong went into the army.[52] In neither case was the departure casual; they were following well-trodden migration routes, recruited by agents with established local networks.[53]

Soldiers could be recruited so easily in soldier-producing regions that recruiters were ready to travel long distances to collect them. There was a traffic in soldiers, a distribution of the local products to regions where soldiers were hard to come by.[54] Recruiters turned up regularly in Caoxian (Shandong), whose 'special product' (*techan*) was soldiers.[55] Shijiazhuang (Hebei) acted as an entrepôt for the soldier trade; young men from neighbouring counties went into the city to meet recruiters from all over China, and then set off for their new life in the army.[56]

Finally there were *garrison towns*, such as Baoding (Hebei) or Xuzhou (Jiangsu) where the military was the main employer and where army service was a natural career for young men. Shen Congwen grew up in a town like this, Chatong (Hunan), a tiny border town on the edge of minority lands. Almost all of its four or five thousand households had a member in the army, or were involved in supplying the army.[57] Shen's father and grandfather had been soldiers; so were he and his brother. In this town there was no division between soldiers and civilians; the two worlds lived together in comfortable harmony.[58]

The regions I have discussed were not the only places where recruits were raised, but they did produce disproportionate numbers of soldiers, and made up for those regions where recruits were hard to find. Non-recruitment regions, besides being more prosperous, were often dominated by the still-pervasive contempt for military service. Li Zongren was the first person in the history of his native Lingui (Guangxi) to choose a military career, and he was harshly criticised for his choice.[59] The scorn for the military career went beyond the traditional respect for literary careers and disparagement of military ones (*zhongwen qingwu*); it involved as well an unarticulated recog-nition that becoming a soldier solved no problems for society, but rather created new ones. This was confirmed by a study done by Chen Zhengmo in the early 1930s which showed that though army recruitment might ease a local surplus of poor peasants, it also created labour shortages, a major problem in parts of Guizhou, Sichuan and Hunan.[60] The shortages were seasonal, but they cut into production, at the same time that the army made ever-growing demands for support on the rural economy. Whether soldiers lived off their native places, or off 'foreign parts', they expected to be maintained at a higher level than they had known before they went into the army. Two sombre comments from the mid 1920s reflect the expectations of peasants-turned-soldiers, and their predatory attitude to the world they had left:

the Chinese peasant or coolie expects to be permitted to prey more or less openly on the unarmed and helpless civilian population within his reach just as soon as he lays aside his carrying-pole or mattock and dons the thin, fading-grey cotton uniform of the soldier.

The majority see in the uniform a license to loot, in the rifle the chance to gain a wealth of sorts; in the roving life of the soldier what little romance there is to be had out of an existence which is at best barren.[61]

2

GOING INTO THE ARMY

Chinese warlord soldiers were mercenaries, but they still had to be
actively recruited; few of them offered their services uninvited.
Recruitment was a continuous process; new men were drawn in from
the civilian world, existing men-at-arms (soldiers, bandits and militiamen) recycled through the armed world. The rate of recruitment
oscillated, highest before a major war or local crisis, declining thereafter as demand fell off, and as the deaths and injuries of battle
deterred potential recruits. Armies used various techniques to get
soldiers, some of them hold-overs from the past, some, products of
the warlord period.

Traditional means of soldier recruitment had relied heavily on
family connections. Under the Qing, sons followed their fathers into the
army. The Manchu Banners were hereditary units in a formal sense;
the Green Standards recruited through an informal system known as
father/son soldiers (*fuzi bing*); when a father had had enough of
military service, his son took his place. Feng Yuxiang replaced his
father at the age of eleven. For the first few years his only duty was to
turn up at roll call and collect his pay. His opium-sodden father had
bequeathed him a valuable sinecure.[1] The hereditary system covered
reserves as well as active soldiers. Bannermen drew small monthly
stipends when not on active duty, which were raised to regular wages
when fighting broke out. These stipends were continued after the fall
of the Qing, even though the Banner units were disbanded.[2]

Familial patterns of recruitment continued into the warlord
period, but the ballooning of army size meant that there were not
enough men from soldier families to fill more than a small proportion
of the openings for soldiers. The hereditary system continued more
as an insurance system for the sons of decrepit soldiers, whose only
legacy was secure employment, than as a major form of recruiting.

Other forms of personal connections became much more important in recruitment. The *personal ties of officers*, their network of connections in their native places, were major channels of recruitment. Ceng Guofan started the practice of direct officer recruitment to meet the emergency of the Taiping Rebellion. He raised the Xiang Army by getting his subordinates to recruit men from their home districts (*tongxiang*), and made use of feelings of local solidarity as a key element in army organisation.[3] The attractions of the system were strong enough to entrench it in recruitment practice throughout the late Qing and into the warlord period. Recruits had the security of serving with a known officer, who in theory would take responsibility for the welfare of a fellow native. Officers got men who 'belonged' to them (*bing wei jiang you*).[4] Since officers normally stood higher in the local social hierarchy than common soldiers, local ties carried connotations of social deference, a natural propensity to accept command, which made the maintenance of military discipline attractively simple.

Recruitment by officers in their native places characterised the best warlord armies. Feng Yuxiang did it routinely. In 1917 he sent his junior officers home on leave with orders to recruit at least ten men in their villages; most of them exceeded their quotas.[5] In 1920, when he was stationed in Changde (Hunan), far away from the Hebei homes of his officers and men, he sent his officers home on rotation to get soldiers (*huijia daibing*).[6] Cai Tingkai habitually recruited in his native Luoding (Guangdong). As a junior officer he went in person; the number of men he recruited rose with his rank – twenty men when he was a lieutenant to a whole company when he was a colonel.[7] Every time he came home for a family visit, he recruited some men, becoming over time a major local job-provider. In 1932, Cai, by then commander of the 19th Route Army, still drew strongly on his native county and province. His training regiment was half Cantonese; six and a half per cent of the men came from Luoding, as did twelve per cent of the officers.[8]

Recruitment through officer connections did not have to involve visits home; an officer could simply send home for men, as the military governor of Guizhou did in 1917, when he had three hundred men sent to him from his native county.[9] Like other commanders who used the system, he knew he would get men he could trust. Soldiers liked the system because, in naturally homogenous units, they were assured of 'mutual friendship, mutual aid and mutual support in time of sickness'.[10] The only wild card in this cosy pack was the officer's sincerity: would he live up to his paternalist commitment or not?

Soldiers recruited through personal ties too. They brought in their relatives and friends, in a form of recruitment which was the military equivalent of civilian chain migration – one migrant drew in a string of later migrants, helping them to leave home, find employment and adjust to the new milieu. Family ties, local ties, secret society ties were all influential in getting recruits to join established (and presumably contented) soldiers. Officers encouraged their men to recruit in this way, because it saved them the trouble and time of recruiting themselves.

This was the problem of personal recruitment. Though it was the surest way of getting reliable troops, it was time-consuming. Personal ties had to be lubricated, and officers had to put themselves out. Many preferred more impersonal forms of recruitment, using *professional agents and entrepreneurs* to get their men.

One common system of recruitment resembled the mercenary systems of medieval Europe in which roving knights (*Landsknechte*) hired themselves and their band of followers to anyone willing to pay them. In warlord China there were men with military training, unemployed officers or men who had attended military school but had never found a permanent commission, who would collect a group of men and hire themselves to existing armies, on the premise that an officer-plus-men was a more attractive recruitment prospect than an officer alone. These men were quintessential mercenaries, despised as 'public prostitutes willing to sell themselves and their men to the highest bidder', or as 'feckless officers' (*xiansan guan*), men devoid of any moral or social scruples.[11] Most of their outfits were small, but some of them grew large, and were known as 'guest armies' (*kejun*), wandering, rootless forces which turned up first in one warlord camp and then in another. Fan Shisheng was a classic example of the type; he fought first in his native Yunnan, then in Guangdong, Guangxi and Jiangxi, never a complete subordinate, but never quite strong enough to be his own master. His calling in life was to provide extra strength for other, more successful commanders.[12]

Military entrepreneurs like Fan supplied themselves with their men; civilian entrepreneurs simply supplied warm bodies to the armies, as labour contractors supplied men to factories or to overseas employers. The civilian entrepreneurs worked established beats, in villages and in the streets and market-places of towns, softening up potential recruits with drinks and free meals, inveigling them into the army. They held no official army commissions as recruiters; they were self-appointed brokers who got hold of young men and sold them into the army. Their incentive was the finder's fee paid for each man delivered to the barracks. The business was lucrative; in Chengdu in the early 1920s the fee per head was 6 *yuan*.[13] This free market system made good money for the entrepreneur, but it tended to produce poor soldiers, inadequate, stupid or naive men, often the dupes of the recruiter. It also cost the commanders money.

An equally painless but cheaper form of recruitment involved commanders in using the resources of local government offices. An example from the mid 1920s shows how this system worked (in theory):

General Chang Chung-chang (Zhang Zongchang) wants 40,000 men out of Shantung province. He sends out an order for that many troops. The province is divided into groups. Each district has a headman. The headman of the districts advise the headman of the various cities, towns and villages in the area that they must produce so many soldiers by a certain date.

The village or city headman calls a meeting of the heads of all the families in his town. He tells them how many men the city must produce. Then they pro-rate the thing. A family of three boys sends two, one with four boys three and so on. They never take a son if he is the only boy in the family... In a few days you have your army of 40,000 men.[14]

This account describes a neat, impartial system, almost a selective service system. The officials are even-handed, the exemptions humanitarian, the load spread evenly. Sometimes the system did work in this way. The gazetteer of Xuanwei (Yunnan) records a carefully regulated process, run from the magistrate's *yamen*. The county maintained its own recruitment office and employed its own recruitment officer (*mubing guan*). Between 50 and 500 men were recruited each year, and sent to join the general recruit pool in the provincial capital. Each recruit got a bonus, which cost the county 40,000 *yuan* over the nineteen years covered in the gazetteer.[15]

More often county authorities cooperated reluctantly with the demands of the military, from a recognition of *force majeure*. A county would receive an order to supply a certain number of men by a certain date, and had no choice but to comply. In 1933, the garrison commander of Xuchang (Henan) ordered the magistrate to get recruits; the order was filled through the *baojia* chiefs, with each recruit getting 30 *yuan* from county funds as a bonus.[16] It was an expensive and troublesome business for the officials; the incidental costs of recruitment – bonuses and transport costs – had to be paid out of their own budgets. In Linqu (Shandong) local authorities had to pay 1,500 *yuan* in one year to finance recruiting.[17] Recruits were not formally conscripted; bonuses encouraged some to volunteer, while others could be picked up at markets or fairs.[18] The one advantage to a locality was that officials could use these forced recruitment drives to get rid of undesirables, to skim off the local scum into the army. Commanders knew this, and used this type of recruitment rarely.[19] A more reliable practice was to recruit directly, off the streets.

Street recruiting was the most visible form of army recruitment in warlord China, and so was often seen as the only form. Recruiting officers on special posting from their units would set up a booth at a street corner, in a market-place, in front of a temple, at a fair. A sign with two bold and widely recognised characters would go up: 'Soldiers wanted' (*zhao bing*).[20] Passers-by, loafers, street kids, any young male would be fed a line by the recruiter, and given visions of a wonderful new life in the army.

Street recruiting operations ranged from one-man efforts to large team efforts. In the major recruitment areas, and in times of crisis, there was often competition between recruiters.[21] In Linqu (Shandong) twelve separate recruiting teams appeared in 1925, each representing a different army.[22] Competition was sometimes fierce, poaching of recruits not uncommon. To get recruits in this competitive atmosphere, recruiters had to do more than put up a sign. In 1913, Feng Yuxiang took over the theatre in Yancheng (Henan), and put on a running entertainment, which incorporated propaganda for army life. Legmen were sent out to scour neighbouring villages for young men, promising them at least entertainment and at most a new life.[23] Wu Peifu launched a major advertising campaign when he was recruiting in Jinan and Caoxian (Shandong) in 1924. The walls of both places were plastered with advertisements to bring in recruits.[24]

This is a description of a similar recruitment drive, from a furious critic:

How are the mercenaries recruited? There on the corner a man with a flag cries 'Soldiers, soldiers'. At once the street is black with people, men in groups run flocking around him. He immediately jots down their names and immediately they are enlisted. It is important to note what part of the people have thus joined the army. It is either the poor whose folly has brought them to want, or the vicious whose ill-conduct has brought them into contempt. On the one hand the poor, having long been underfed, ill-clothed and filthily lodged in their dwellings, are sickly and weak to the last degree. On the other the vicious, having been given to conspiracy, violence and mischief, retain still their ill-nature and wickedness. The former ought to be in their graves, the latter ought to have been cast into prison. But instead they are both in the army.[25]

The high-flown moralism of the writer (a Chinese journalist who must have been trained by missionaries) reflected the widespread belief that street recruiting swept into the army the scum of the civilian world, the *canaille*, the riff-raff, the layabouts, the 'market-place bums' (*shijing liumin*).[26] The impression was reinforced by the speed at which street recruiting took place; there were plenty of candidates around to respond to recruiters' calls. In five days of street recruiting, Feng Yuxiang got a whole battalion, in Jingxian (Zhili).[27] Such ease of recruitment was routine, at least in the regions known to produce soldiers. Recruitment took place so often that men who were already dissatisfied with their lives and had decided to go into the army simply hung around until a sign went up.

This is confirmed by the fact that although street recruiting usually took place in towns or cities, the bulk of recruits were peasants. Potential recruits were men who had already detached themselves from rural life, or had been evicted from it, and had drifted into the towns.

The casual sweeping up of men for the army would suggest that recruiters were not particular about the *calibre of recruits*, provided they were physically mobile. In fact the better units were concerned about recruit quality, and did have minimum physical and moral standards. In the late Qing, the Newly Created Army required that its recruits be at least 5ft in height, able to lift 100 lb and to walk twenty *li* in an hour; the weak, the sickly, opium addicts and men with poor eyesight were disqualified.[28] (If the 5ft height requirement seems short, it should be compared with the minimum height for British soldiers at the same time – 5ft 3in, a height not reached by thirty per cent of recruits.[29])

Twenty years later the Ministry of War's requirements were higher:[30] 'Recruits for the army must be between 20 and 25 years of age, must be at least 5 ft. 6 ins. (except in the southern provinces where the minimum is 5 ft. 4 ins.), must be free from physical defects and must be able to lift 133 lbs.'

These requirements were formal, and probably seldom observed. Feng Yuxiang, who prided himself on the calibre of his men, was satisfied with less. He took men between the ages of 18 and 25, between 5 ft and 5 ft 5 in with no scars.[31] Many armies would take anyone who was not a cripple, regardless of height, strength – or age. Very young boys were often recruited. Shen Congwen was only thirteen when he enlisted, and soon became one of the youngest sergeants ever.[32] Deng Baosan was fifteen on enlistment.[33] The physical characteristics of recruits were measured less in terms of size and height than of general endurance. Chinese soldiers were not supposed to look impressive, unless they were personal guards to a commander. But they did need to be tough enough to withstand maltreatment, resist disease and recover from wounds without medical attention. Physical durability (*chiku nailao*) was far more important than brawn.[34]

Desirable moral attributes in soldiers hinged around family background, personal character and education. The Newly Created Army refused to take men of no fixed abode, men without established family connections and men with criminal records.[35] The Ministry of War's regulations (1916) went further:[36] 'They [recruits] must be residents of the locality in which they enlist, and must be able to furnish satisfactory particulars regarding their families. Opium smokers, law breakers and other undesirable characters are not accepted.' Feng Yuxiang, less ambitious than the Ministry, insisted only that his recruits be of good family (*liangmin*).[37] The standards elsewhere were lower, and they declined over time. By the mid 1920s, as a report from Rongxian (Sichuan) indicated, there were none at all in some parts of China:[38] 'Until recently recruits had to furnish a guarantor, but now any applicant is accepted, without a surety and no questions asked.' Education was even harder to guarantee than good family background or moral probity. Except for a brief period at the end of the Qing, educated soldiers were a rarity. That brief period was the six years between the abolition of the examination system in 1905 and the Revolution of 1911, when the old education system was moribund and the new system had not emerged. During this period, the educational levels of ordinary recruits were often very high. As a child Chen Guofu watched his uncle, a major in the Hunan provincial army, enlist new recruits. Almost all of them had five to six years' education in private academies, while ten per cent were already *xiucai*, graduates of the first level of the examination system.[39] The Hubei New Army of the same period would enlist only men who were already literate.[40] These recruits were young men whose prospects for advancement through the traditional route had been stymied, and who were too poor to go and study abroad. For them the new armies represented one of the few career choices.

Educational standards were never as high again. Bright young men who were slightly younger gravitated to the new military schools, and became officers rather than common soldiers. New career prospects for the literate opened up in business and industry. Commanders came to accept that they could not ask for educated recruits. Zhang Zuolin would have liked his men to have completed their primary school education, but he settled for the possession of 'common sense'.[41] The ranks were not a place for men with education. Shen Congwen went into the army with little education, his schooling interrupted by truancy. Though he acquired a rudimentary knowledge of classical Chinese through working in his unit office, he left the army at twenty, convinced it was no place for an educated man: army life was conducive only to card playing, story telling, drinking and opium smoking.[42]

During the warlord period the calibre of soldiers sank far below the standards of the late Qing New Armies. This might seem to suggest that the army became a less and less attractive career, until it appealed only to the basest elements in society. The truth is probably rather different, and has to do with availability, rather than straightforward attraction. The New Armies were deliberately designed to bring in a new type of soldier, to raise the standards of Chinese armies; during the period of their formation, there was little competition for capable people.[43] Once new employment avenues opened up, the military had to compete, and had to take anyone available for service. Moral, spiritual, educational and physical characteristics were less important than willingness to serve.

Recruitment normally means bringing new men into the army; in China it also meant recycling those who were already in the armed world – soldiers, bandits, militiamen. The practice of *recruiting serving soldiers* went back to the practices of the Huai Army, in the 1860s; that army enlisted men from the disbanded Xiang Army, from the Ever-Victorious Army and even from Taiping units.[44] The Huai Army in its turn provided recruits for the Newly Created Army.[45] During the warlord period the practice intensified. Sometimes men were lured away from their units by promises of better pay; sometimes they were picked up from the battlefield. Defeated, scattered soldiers (*sanbing*) were at the end of their military careers only if they chose to leave the army. Their officers might take themselves off to the safety of a foreign concession or a monastery; the men would often hang around, hoping to be incorporated into the victor's army.[46] In 1924, Zhou Yinren raised fifty per cent of a new army from the force of a man he had just defeated.[47] *Sanbing* were also collected by commanders who had not been involved in a specific battle. In 1925 Hu Jingyi rushed recruiters to corral the defeated soldiers of Cao Gun, though he himself had taken no part in Cao's downfall.[48]

This form of recruitment was satisfactory, to both commanders and men. The men avoided disbandment and the loss of livelihood, and the commanders got experienced soldiers. They also got genuine turncoats, men whose loyalty was to their paymaster. (Chinese soldiers did not have to turn their coats or change their uniforms literally, since most wore interchangeable grey cotton uniforms; all that had to be changed were armbands and insignia.[49]) For this reason, defeated soldiers were not recruited by the better armies. Feng Yuxiang generally made a point of refusing them, but even he weakened when his need was great. In 1924, at the height of his expansion, he recruited 20,000 defeated soldiers of Wu Peifu.[50]

Soldiers made the easiest recruits for an expanding army; they did not have to be trained, or acculturated to army life. They did present some problems, however. Aside from their dubious loyalties, they could be difficult to command; they were more experienced in army life, and less likely to put up with maltreatment than raw recruits. These drawbacks apart, recruitment of *sanbing* had great attractions, to the civilian as well as to the military world. Taking them under a new command prevented them from becoming bandits, or from gravitating into the cities where, if they still had their guns, they were a major nuisance. Wuhan, like other cities, ran periodic sweeps to round up *sanbing* who were causing trouble on the streets.[51] It was simpler if the armies took them in.

A few of the former soldiers who found new commanders during the warlord period were foreigners, White Russians. After the October Revolution, White Russians poured into Manchuria and North China, some of them soldiers of the Tsarist armies, willing to work as bouncers, bodyguards or as regular soldiers. Zhang Zong-chang had a White Russian unit in his army until his demise in 1928.[52] So did Zhang Zuolin. In 1925, an American marine unit bivouacked near Tianjin encountered a Russian unit:

On big Manchurian ponies, well fed, well shod, well trained, came a troop of horsemen. The troopers' uniforms were of such a dark green that at first glance they looked black. They wore high, yellow leather boots. Each man carried a lance, the butt of which rested in a leather socket near his left stirrup, the nib of which flaunted itself high over his head and bore a flutter-ing pennant. Each man at his waist wore a long-barreled Mauser pistol in a wooden holster. Each man also carried a dadao, the beheading knife which looks like a machete.[53]

These immaculately turned-out soldiers were Russians, the last remnants of a military tradition whose fascination with martial glamour over military efficiency had brought it to defeat.

Militia units and irregular armies (minjun) also provided recruits for regular armies. They had enough military experience to make them seem to be good candidates for the army. There were vast numbers of such men available, especially militiamen. In some provinces they outnumbered soldiers; in Sichuan (1932) there were between half a million and a million militiamen for 300,000 to 380,000 soldiers.[54] In other provinces the numbers were roughly at parity; Fujian (1932) had 40,000 militiamen for 50,000 soldiers.[55]

Systematic recruitment of soldiers from militia units was a key form of recruitment in the Taiping period. Li Hongzhang raised the Huai Army in large part from members of the Anhui militias.[56] In doing so he had full cooperation from the local gentry who had orig-inally raised the militias. By the warlord period the situation was different. Local leaders who raised militias (*mintuan* in the country-side, *shangtuan* in the cities and towns) wanted them to protect their own interests, often against marauding soldiers. When a warlord tried to recruit militiamen, he ran up against local opposition.[57]

Resistance to militia recruitment stimulated army commanders to recruit them by stealth or by force. In 1924 Hu Jingyi 'borrowed' one of the militia units of Guangcong (Hebei); he never returned it.[58] In Fujian, the fighters of militia units had such a high reputation (they were hereditary units) that local commanders would even try to press-gang them.[59] Militia sponsors who had put money into raising a force to protect themselves were usually outraged at army attempts to commandeer their men, but army commanders were impervious. They recognised good soldier material. Even Mao Zedong saw the potential of militiamen. He advocated their recruitment into the peasant movement forces in Hunan (1927): 'Taking over these old armed forces is one way in which peasants may build up their own forces.'[60]

The recruitment of irregular forces (*minjun*) is a mysterious matter because the irregular units were themselves so nebulous. They appeared as formal fighting units only in times of acute upheaval, as in Guangdong in 1912, when 50,000 *minjun* appeared – and then just as suddenly disappeared again.[61] Some of them were bandits, some secret society members, some local toughs. Serving as 'irregulars' was only an interlude in their normal careers. When the interlude was over, they could be recruited into regular forces, or could melt back into the armed fringes of society from which they came.

The most important paramilitary source of soldiers was one very close to the 'irregulars' – *bandits*. The intimate relationship between the army and bandit worlds is discussed in chapter 5. As we shall see there, bandits were frequently recruited into armies, so much so that the distinction between soldiers and bandits was often one of name only. It took a long while even for the Red Army to rectify the names. When Otto Braun (Li De) first arrived in Jiangxi in 1932, he found 'unhealthy influences' still widespread in the Red Army, some from 'old military traditions' and some from 'the practices of former robbers'.[62] The Red Army at least had the advantage of believing itself to be a furnace which would melt down and remould men of even the most undesirable origins.[63] Other armies knew that bandits would change little in service.

Going into the army

Recruitment in warlord China involved a constant search for new recruits and a constant recycling of men under arms. China's armies were major employers. Until 1937, there was no problem in finding men; the dislocation of the traditional rural economy and the slow growth of new forms of employment meant that there were plenty of willing recruits. The army was a growth industry.

3

LIFE IN THE ARMY

'A soldier's life is terrible hard' says Alice.[1]

Enlisting as a soldier is one thing; living in the army is another. Armies make great demands on recruits to adjust and adapt to their new life. 'Few organisations place as much stress on assimilating as does the military establishment.'[2] New soldiers must submit to military discipline, stop thinking of themselves as civilians and identify with the army. A soldier's theoretical *raison d'être* is to fight; he can only do this if he is disciplined, obedient and able to function as part of a hierarchy. Armies have the means to make their men acculturate. The system of ranks makes men legally superior or inferior, empowered to give commands or forced to accept them. Men who balk at the system are punished, as severely and as arbitrarily as the commander sees fit.

Officers have the power to command and to punish, but they are not the primary agents of acculturation to army life. For the new recruit, the voice of the army is the non-commissioned officer, the sergeant whose job it is to knock the newcomer into shape and make him a functioning soldier. He is responsible for initiation to army life, for the inculcation of *esprit de corps*, for making the recruit into a new being, cut off from his origins and incorporated into a separate world.

In the armies of warlord China, initiation into army life lacked the extremes of harshness reached in the German or Japanese armies. Most recruits were mercenaries, and mercenaries, if they were going to stay, had to be better treated than conscripts. Desertion was easy; the unhappy recruit could go over the wall rather than suffer. With self-designated misfits removed, those who stayed needed less pressure to fit in. In any case, China's military tradition did not contain the concept of a harsh induction process. The Qing armies were recruited largely through hereditary means; soldiers' sons did not have to make major adjustments from a civilian to a military world. The lack of a tradition of harshness was complemented by a shortage of the bullying, sadistic sergeants hated by recruits elsewhere. Chinese N.C.O.s did not constitute a clear intermediate grouping between officers and men as N.C.O.s did in the armies of other countries; they were simply experienced, long-serving soldiers, who might, in some of the best armies, have received a special training course, but who probably had only seniority to distinguish them from other soldiers.[3]

Even if milder than in other countries, the process of adjustment to army life was still traumatic enough to overwhelm some recruits. A young man who called himself Warrior (*Wufu*) was shocked to the depths of his being when he enlisted in a Guomindang unit in 1934. For him the army was a nightmare. His uniform was coarse and scratchy, and constantly soaked with sweat. Beatings were routine and ghastly; the sight of a soldier being beaten unconscious revolted him. The sleeping conditions were foul, with seventy men sleeping on the floor in a single room. The food was terrible, *mantou* (steamed bread) and water flavoured with soy sauce. There was no medical care and on top of everything else there were eight hours of drill a day. For this young man, an educated youth who had enlisted out of patriotic desire to fight the Japanese, the army was too much. Within three weeks he was out, sprung by his influential family.[4] Less well-connected young men either deserted or stayed, to go through the first stage of army life, basic training.

Basic training varied greatly from army to army. A few armies had special training regiments for recruits, but most trained them alongside existing soldiers. Few could afford extensive weapons training, because of a scarcity of weapons and ammunition, so the stress had to be on drill. Some commanders, like Wu Peifu, were very keen on training their men in marching, especially goose-stepping, presenting arms (even if they were wooden dummies), saluting and standing at attention.[5] Other commanders trained their men to fight; Li Zongren was proud of the fact that although his men looked sloppy, and could not keep step, they were superb fighters.[6] At the lower levels of the warlord military hierarchy, little attention was given either to parade-ground smartness or to fighting skills; giving a man a uniform and a gun was enough to make him a soldier.

Those armies that did take training seriously usually reinforced it

37

with some form of indoctrination, to make men identify with their unit. (This was distinct from political training, which was only used in the best Guomindang armies during the Northern Expedition, and in the Red Army.) Feng Yuxiang used a wide, eclectic range of indoctrination techniques, from catechisms and Socratic dialogues to inspirational songs and hymns, including the most appropriate of all, a Chinese version of 'Onward Christian soldiers'.[7]

Lists of 'dos and don'ts' appeared frequently as part of the indoctrination; they were creeds, of the kind immortalised by the Red Army in the Three/Eight Working Style (*sanba zuofeng*). Guomindang armies on the Northern Expedition were taught the 'Ten No Fears' (*shi bu pa*):

Don't fear death   Don't fear hunger
Don't fear poverty   Don't fear tiredness
Don't fear cold   Don't fear distances
Don't fear pain   Don't fear height
Don't fear heat   Don't fear danger.[8]

By the time of the Anti-Japanese War instructions were less inspirational and more cold-blooded. The 'Three Don'ts and Three Believes' taught the soldiers the following:

Don't disobey orders   Believe in the ideology
Don't retreat if wounded Believe in the leader
Don't submit if captured   Believe in your commander.[9]

This preoccupation with numbers reached its most extreme with the 'Soldier's Ten Commandments', published in a Guomindang soldiers' magazine in 1948:

Fire *one* rifle
Carry *two* hundred bullets
Eat *three* bowls of rice
Keep watch on all *four* sides
Wake up for reveille at *five* o'clock
Reach your objective in the *sixth* month
Break through *seven* rings of defence
March *eighty* li
Survive *nine* narrow escapes
Put up with total (*shifen*) difficulty.[10]

This litany was certainly written by a joker – but it was a parody of what was actually taught.

Assimilation of recruits was not dependent solely on ideological training, nor on drill or weapons training. The pressure to conform, to assimilate to the army, came not from army command but from the recruit's barracks companions, the old soldiers. The 'old brothers' (*lao xiongdi*) were the most influential figures in the young soldier's life. 'The officers controlled the old brothers, and the old brothers controlled us', lamented the unhappy Warrior.[11] In the enforced intimacy of barracks and army camps, the newcomer soon learnt who was in charge and whom he had to please. The pressure to fit in was strong; it came not only from the seasoned soldiers, but also from the recruit's internal needs – the army was his surrogate family.

There are very few statistics on the age and marital status of soldiers, but those that do exist indicate that they were young and unmarried. Tao Menghe's survey of a Shanxi Guards Brigade made in 1929 showed that over fifty per cent of the men in the survey were under 25, and that seventy-three per cent were unmarried.[12] Statistics collected by the Training Regiment of Cai Tingkai's 19th Route Army in 1932 gave an average age for soldiers of 24.[13] Even those soldiers who were married would only have their families with them if they were still stationed in their native district, and then not in the barracks; no army had married quarters. Being away from home, young and unmarried created a compulsion to develop a variant form of emotional warmth in the comradeship of the army. To supplement comradeship, there were the privileges that came to a man with a gun. Recruits quickly came to share with established soldiers the attractive pastimes the army permitted them.

In almost all armies, forms of behaviour are licensed which are considered depraved and intolerable in civilian society. 'The military establishment is an all-male culture which informally tolerates behavioural excesses to a greater degree than mixed civilian society.'[14] In the barracks, the pressure from mothers, wives and neighbours to behave is replaced by the diametrically opposed pressure to conform to the norm of the tough, swaggering, vice-loving fighter.

Most Chinese armies observed the convention of discipline on duty and licence off. The very few armies, such as Feng Yuxiang's, which enforced strict discipline at all times were famous just for the fact that they were exceptions.

Army authorities condoned all forms of licence – gambling, opium smoking, consorting with prostitutes and drinking – and army life provided enough free time to indulge in them. Besides free time the army gave its men the uniforms and weapons which were the means to demand or to take by force the pleasures they wanted. Whether a soldier paid or not for what he got depended on his own conscience or on his officer's command. Most were impervious to the dictates of conscience; very few had moral standards imposed upon them by their officers.

Some officers actually supplied their soldiers' pleasures to them directly. Zhu Zhixin described a unit in which the officers procured prostitutes to work in the barracks and ran gambling tables for men whose tastes ran to money rather than sex.[15] The men got their rest and relaxation without having to seek it out, and the officers got back a good part of the men's wages.

Entertainment for soldiers was laid on by other organisations too, usually to try and keep them off the streets. In Guiyang (Guizhou) the city authorities put on theatricals for the local soldiers (1923):

In order to keep them profitably employed, they are treated to tea and cakes at the theatre daily while watching theatricals. The officers have more solid refreshment while engaging in the same pasttime in the public park.[16]

Christian missionaries in Jinan (Shandong) opened a soldiers' reading-room in 1913, where soldiers could read edifying volumes put out by the Christian Literature Society, or listen to the good news in the lecture hall.[17] For most soldiers, however, entertainment did not mean tea and tiny cakes, theatricals or good news; it meant opium, sex, gambling and drinking.

Opium smoking varied in degree in the army as it did in civilian life. The Yunnanese armies were notorious for addiction; it was inevitable in a province where opium grew prolifically, and where soldiers were regularly assigned to guard opium caravans.[18] In the opium-growing regions, and along the opium routes, addiction was standard. Elsewhere, specific units were riddled with the drug. All the adults in the pre-revolutionary army world in which Feng Yuxiang's father served were addicts, including both his parents.[19] The Anhui provincial forces just after the 1911 Revolution were known as 'twin-pipe armies' (*shuang qiang jun*), because the soldiers all carried opium pipes (*yanqiang*) along with their rifles (*buqiang*).[20]

Sexual indulgence could be found in acceptable form, from society's point of view, with prostitutes. Prostitution was an important industry, employing hundreds of thousands of women forced into the profession by economic necessity, by personal misfortune or by their own inclination. In Beijing in 1918 there were 450 brothels, and 10,000 prostitutes.[21] The most expensive catered to the foreign military; for the cheaper ladies, soldiers were a very important part of their clientele. Some armies had their own camp followers, but most used local resources. To the general public, prostitution was sordid but unavoidable; prostitutes were professionals who paid the price for their depravity by being ostracised. Their activities were discreetly welcomed, because they diverted the lusts of soldiers away from respectable women, and reduced the risk of the most frightful form of soldier licence, rape.

Rape was too appalling to mention publicly. Chinese sources make veiled references to 'the peril of women', and to soldiers 'bothering' women; foreign sources speak of 'unmentionable horrors'. The fear of rape was universal, and soldiers were the prime objects of fear as rapists.[22] Whether they were or not is impossible to prove, since no statistics on such a dreadful subject exist.

Gambling was a regionalised form of licence. Cantonese soldiers were the greatest gamblers, taking their provincial passion with them wherever they were stationed. An indignant missionary in Ganzhou (Jiangxi) reported after the arrival of Cantonese troops in 1922 that 'every street is full of soldiers, and all the principal streets are lined with gambling tables. This has been unknown in the city before.'[23]

Drinking was a less important pastime in Chinese armies than it was in the armies of most other countries. Vodka was the staple of the Russian army, taken internally to deaden sorrows, and externally to disinfect wounds or treat frost-bite. The drinking of British soldiers was exceeded only by that of their officers. As Florence Nightingale remarked tartly, 'if the facilities for washing were as great as those for drinking, our Indian Army would be the cleanest body of men in the world'.[24] Florence Nightingale managed to reform some of the bad aspects of the British Army, but not the drinking. Chinese soldiers drank, but not in the quantity or with the regularity of soldiers of other nations.

The eager pursuit of pleasures which the civilian world denied its members was regarded by soldiers as one of the perks of military service. They tried to enjoy themselves on duty or off. Licence was mainly off duty. Travel was mainly on. Travel on foot was usually enjoyed only by soldiers who were tourists at heart. Li Zongren was; he recorded his first campaigns into the lush beauty of southern Hunan more as travelogues than as campaign records, with detailed descriptions of the beauty spots he saw.[25] Travel by train or by boat was more generally appreciated. The journeys were free; ticket sellers did not make trouble for men with guns, nor did passengers whose seats or berths were taken. In areas of constant military movement, such as the West River system in Guangxi and Guangdong, or the railway system of North China, operators accepted glumly that soldiers took precedence over other traffic. Warlords fought over control of waterways and railways; their men rode about on them:[26] 'The soldiers appear to indulge in unlimited periods of leave, regarding this section of the railway [Tianjin-Dezhou] as their private property. They spend their days in hectic joy-riding.'

Free travel was one of the fringe benefits that army service brought over and above the fundamental reward of army service, pay. Mercenaries were attracted to the army by the prospect of pay, and stayed as wage soldiers. The question of pay was complex and deceptive. Formal wage scales existed, and were presumably known to soldiers and to potential recruits. Here is a sample:[27]

	Sergeant	Corporal	First Class Private	2nd Class Private
Beijing, 1915	—	4.8 *taels*	4.5 *taels*	4.2 *taels*
Guangzhou, 1926	16 *yuan*	14 *yuan*	10.5 *yuan*	10 *yuan*
Guangxi, 1926	12 *yuan*	—	10 *yuan*	—
Taiyuan, 1929	9 *yuan*	8 *yuan*	7 *yuan*	6.3 *yuan*

These were monthly wages. What they represented is less straightforward than the bald amounts suggest. First of all, the value depended on whether the wages were paid in paper currency, which might have little exchange value, or in metal currency.[28] Tight-fisted or hard-pressed commanders could resort to printing their own paper currency, or to debasing metal currency, to pay their soldiers. In 1927, Feng Yuxiang, finding his treasury depleted to 500 silver dollars, had $20,000,000 of paper money printed. This 'military currency' (*junyong liutong zhuan*) was all 'backed' by $500.[29] This

payment in paper money was seldom an acceptable practice from the
soldiers' point of view; even if the money could be forced on civilians,
soldiers liked the feel of real money – silver.[30] Even more important
was whether they were paid at all. Arrears of pay were standard, and
were the single most important cause of mutinies. Twenty-six out of
eighty mutinies recorded between 1911 and 1922 were protests
against non-payment of wages.[31]

Unpaid soldiers were like time-bombs. A skilled commander could
judge their mood closely enough to pay them just before they
exploded. The garrison troops at Liuan (Anhui) got their back pay in
1915 as soon as they started minor blazes, a sure sign that a major explosion was imminent.[32] This primitive approach was not always
adequate; when it failed, soldiers took their wages in kind, not from
their delinquent commanders but from civilians, through loot.

The irregularity and unreliability of soldiers' pay did not threaten
their survival. Even if they were not paid, they were fed and housed.
Commanders understood without having heard it Napoleon's
dictum that 'an army marches on its stomach'. They kept the supply
of food going. The unit in which Cai Tingkai served in 1919 was not
paid for a whole year, but never went short of food.[33] Li Zongren, in
the first, tenuous stages of his independent command, was seldom
able to pay his men, but he always fed them.[34] An unpaid labourer
would starve; an unpaid soldier still ate.

Soldiers had other sources of income besides pay (see appendix 3).
Battle bonuses were common. Pre-battle bonuses, what the Germans
describe as 'tremble money' (*Zittergeld*), were routine in armies not
fired with zeal. Shen Congwen's unit received one dollar (Mex.) per
man before going off on an anti-bandit campaign.[35] For the victors,
post-battle rewards were also lucrative. In a small operation in 1913,
Cai Tingkai got a cash reward of five *yuan* from his commander, and
'found' another five in the pocket of a dead bandit.[36] The few hours'
fighting netted him more than a month's pay.

Soldiers could also supplement their pay by moonlighting. The in-
dustrious soldier could practise his civilian skills in the army, on his
own account. Literate men could write letters for their comrades,
cobblers could make shoes. Cai Tingkai went bankrupt as a civilian
tailor; in the army he doubled his pay by making uniforms in his
spare time.[37]

Soldiers acquired in the army items which could easily be con-

43

verted into cash: their uniforms and their guns. These were what guaranteed a soldier power over civilians, so they were sold only when he was leaving the army. A Sichuanese deserter in 1926 sold his uniform jacket and pawned his trousers; the yield was enough to replace them with civilian clothing.[38] Guns were much more valuable. The demand for them was high, and anything would sell, with or without ammunition, in working condition or broken. When Cai Tingkai deserted in 1917, he sold his gun for 80 *yuan*, almost a year's pay and enough to finance a three-month rest in Guangzhou plus a cash payment to his wife to keep the family farm going.[39] In 1920, Li Zongren, in desperate financial straits and unable to pay his troops, just managed to stop his fractious men from selling their guns for 200 *yuan* each, and sold some of them himself instead to feed the company.[40]

The ultimate fringe benefit for soldiers was their special status as purchasers. For them, regular market prices did not exist. They could pay what they liked for goods and services. Suppliers recognised superior force and took whatever was offered for meals, prostitutes, or goods.

With all these fringe benefits, the actual amount of army pay lost its significance. Nominal pay might only be a small part of actual income, which was just as well since a soldier seldom saw all of that. Many armies made substantial deductions from pay. Sometimes they were low enough to leave a soldier with a significant cash wage. Shen Congwen earned six *yuan* a month as a young soldier, of which he kept four.[41] Other soldiers were less fortunate. The theoretical pay of a private in the Beiyang Army (1906) was four and a half ounces of silver a month; but the army deducted money for food, uniform, blankets, lamps, curtains, window paper and umbrellas, leaving the soldier with a few copper cash in wages every month.[42] In 1923 soldiers in Guangxi lost almost all their four *yuan* to deductions.[43] A decade later, soldiers in Zhenjiang (Jiangsu) received less than one *yuan* a month; the rest of their pay was deducted for food, uniforms, laundry, compulsory savings and income tax.[44] A general estimate for deductions in the early 1930s was that soldiers lost about three-quarters of their 8–10 *yuan* wages.[45]

For single men who were making no contributions to their families, the vagaries of army pay were tolerable. Their physical needs were taken care of. For married men, or men who were sending money home, the reliability of pay was much more important. As noted above, the information on the marital status of soldiers is very limited. The statistics from the Shanxi training brigade showed that seventy-three per cent were unmarried, and over half of the married men had no children. Sixty-three per cent of the men over 25 were still unmarried, and virtually unmarriageable.[46] But dependents included parents as well as wives and children. Twenty-five per cent of the unmarried men were only sons, with a clear responsibility to support their parents.[47] In fact, two-thirds of the men surveyed did send money home, in small sums. They ranged between one and four *yuan* a month, a supplement to a family income rather than a complete support.[48]

The situation of soldiers' dependents was precarious. When a man was not the major or sole support of his family, his cash contribution was useful. Families of garrison troops were relatively secure. In Shen Congwen's home town of Chatong (Hunan), soldiers' relations came to the barracks once a month to pick up cash and a free allotment of grain. They were also allowed to cultivate rent-free military reserve land.[49] But the families of men serving away from home had to rely on postal remittances. Provided there was money to send, it got through. The Post Office was one of the very few institutions in warlord China which continued to function on a national scale. Mail carriers got through every kind of turmoil, and delivered the mail intact, even when it contained postal drafts, which could easily be converted into cash.

The dependents of absent soldiers generally had a thin time. If they had no other source of income than the soldiers' wages, it was particularly hard. Cai Tingkai's energetic wife tried to support herself and a flock of children and siblings on the proceeds of their tiny farm, with little financial help from him. In one six-month period he sent her 30 *yuan*, but for the next year could manage nothing at all, because he was not paid.[50] Except for the fact that he managed to get leave to help her out at planting and harvest, she would probably have become destitute before his promotions turned her into an affluent officer's wife.

Armies sometimes had formal regulations on the books for the care of soldiers' dependents, such as those published by the Ministry of War in 1915:

Arrangements have been made for the payment of a proportion of soldiers' wages to their families direct, and the latter are excused certain taxes and are ordered to be specially protected by the local officials while the soldier is on service... Pensions are to be paid to the families of those who die in action and to soldiers who are wounded or serve for a long period.[51]

Like many other regulations they remained on paper. Feng Yuxiang was praised just because he did take care of his soldiers' families. Payments were sent regularly, through army channels, and special arrangements were made for families in difficulties. In 1920, when drought struck Hebei, he gave special leave and a sum of money to any Hebei native who wanted to go home to help his family.[52] He also looked after the families of fallen soldiers. In 1923, a family whose son had been killed in battle received 230 *yuan* (and a letter of condolence) a month after his death.[53] In other armies families were lucky to be notified of a soldier's death, let alone to receive compensation.

With the vagaries of soldiers' wages, it might seem that army service was not profitable, that a soldier was not much better off than a civilian. But if one assumes that the majority of soldiers would probably have been employed at the bottom of rural wage scales, or would have earned a small income from a tiny plot of land, their situation looks better. A study published in 1930 which used a wide range of existing statistical material gave a wage range for yearly labourers (*changgong*) of from 6 *yuan* (in parts of Shandong) to 50 *yuan* (in parts of Jiangsu). The lowest wages included board, the highest ones did not. Between the two extremes the majority of figures were clustered in the 20–30 *yuan* region.[54] These were figures for a year's work. However miserable or irregular soldiers' wages were, they were never as low as that.

Another factor made army incomes more attractive than farm ones. In the army there was a pay scale, and pay rose with promotion. An ambitious and capable man could move ahead fast. Luo Binghui enlisted in the Yunnan army in 1915, was promoted three times in six months, and saw his wages rise from 3 to 12 *yuan* a month.[55] After four years in the army, Liu Ruming was able to buy four *mou* of land for his family, at the age of 20.[56] These two men were exceptionally able, but success stories like theirs, unthinkable for a farm boy, were common enough to create the image of great opportunity in the army. Soldiers had some hope; the rural and urban poor had very little. In his short story 'Construction' ('Jianshe') Shen

Congwen looked at the life of soldiers through the eyes of coolies building their barracks:

Because of military discipline, it seemed that the soldiers' chances of being punished or beaten were greater than the workers'. When a man working nearby, carrying a plank or rolling a lead pipe, saw a soldier being punished, having to stand at attention for hours on end on the parade ground at the bottom of the hill, rigid as a board, he found the sight ridiculous. As far as rules were concerned, a worker was much better off; unless he wrecked something, he couldn't be punished; he only had to work flat out. The soldiers seemed to be storing up their energy for the future; their exertion was limited. It was all the rules a soldier had to obey which gave him problems. The first thing a soldier had to know was that whatever happened, his superior officer was always right, and had the right to impose any punishment he saw fit. The soldier had to know all the rules about daily life, about behaviour, uniforms and messing. He didn't have to be intelligent, he didn't have to be stupid either; he didn't have to be inspired, but he did have to believe that everything he did was for the country, or some such double-talk. He had to go out and kill other men bravely, and even more bravely bear someone else sticking a bayonet in his chest. But though there were times when the workers, hauling bricks and grabbling in the mud, mocked the soldiers' life, there were many more times when they envied those men who had some chances. The soldiers didn't really understand how the workers went on with their lives uncomplaining, nor did the workers understand why the soldiers went on as they did. All they knew was that when they saw these young fellows in clean cotton uniforms running around on the parade ground, drilling endlessly in the name of the revolution or some better cause, they had the chance of presenting arms at the station to welcome some V.I.P., to stand rocklike at attention whatever was going on. They also knew that when the soldiers died they had the chance to become heroes, to have their names carved on war memorials, or, if they weren't killed, to get a pile of rewards. When their unit entered a newly captured town, it would be welcomed respectfully by merchants and people. The soldiers would be considered men of standing. To be a man of standing meant to have one's food and clothing provided, not to have to go hungry, not to have to dig in the mud, to pour sweat, to burn with fever or die of cholera. A man who was a labourer today would be doing the same work tomorrow; if you signed on for 30 cents today, you would be working for the same amount next year. The workers' envy for the grey-clad soldiers was obvious.[57]

Life in the army had many drawbacks; it could be harsh, insecure and dangerous. Soldiers could be killed or wounded, and a wound was often a delayed death sentence. They were treated harshly by their officers, cut off from their families. Their living conditions were squalid, they were hated by civilians. For all that, there were many compensations. Soldiers were not overworked, and they had plenty of opportunities for recreation and the enjoyment of vice. They were always fed and often paid. They could loot and plunder. They shared a comradeship with their fellow-soldiers which was often warm and comforting. After he left the army for the competitive world of the Beijing intelligentsia, Shen Congwen looked back with nostalgia to the good fellowship of the self-enclosed world of the army.[58] Army life did not suit all young men. But for the tough and adventurous it offered an existence which made civilian life look drab and monotonous. For the less bold, there were also large advantages. Peng Yuting, the social critic and reformer, once remarked rather sourly that 'except for eating and drinking, doing one's job, getting drunk and sleeping, there are no psychological rewards in army life'.[59] Given that these pastimes represented as much as many poor young men could dream of, he must have been joking when he seemed to disparage them. Compared to the misery of peasant life, the army was very comfortable.

This was the irony of warlordism – army life was good enough to keep China's armies growing, and thus to perpetuate the tyranny of soldiers.

4

OFFICERS AND MEN

In any army, a large body of men is commanded by a small corps
of officers. The degree of separation between the two groups is determined by the officers' attitudes towards their men. Since command is
vertical, from top to bottom, it cannot depend on the men. Officer–
men relations usually mirror the larger society from which the army
is drawn. In warlord China, where social flux was acute, this mirror
effect meant that more than one pattern existed simultaneously.

Societies with a strong hereditary social hierarchy tend to produce
armies in which there is a *caste separation* between officers and men. In
the pre-Second World War British, German and Japanese armies it
was the right and duty of a proportion of the sons of the social elite to
serve as officers. These young men were born to lead as their men
were born to follow. 'Soldiers accorded officers the respect due to
rank and title.'[1] This pattern was alien to China. The Qing military
caste, the Manchus, encompassed officers and men, and was quite
distinct from the Han civil elite. The hereditary officer corps of the
Han Green Standards was devoid of any social standing. The nearest
approximation to a caste separation between officers and men was
found in the Xiang and Huai Armies. In those armies commanders
who belonged to the elite by virtue of their birth and their talents
recruited soldiers who were their inferiors within local social
hierarchies. But these officers were not professional military men;
they were scholar-officials who became officers to meet a military
emergency.[2]

In societies whose predominant pattern of social organisation is
democratic or socialist, officers and men are all servants of the state.
There is a separation between officers and men, but it is based on a
distinction of function, not of social origin. In ideal form, this is the con-
ception of officer–men relations in the U.S. Army, or the Israeli
Army. It was unknown in China before the rise of the Red Army, the

first force to be based on an ideology which denied traditional social hierarchies, and which explicitly made the army subordinate to the dominant institution, the Party.

One of the major forms of officer–men relations in warlord China was a *contractual relationship*. A mercenary commander made a contract (usually unwritten, but sometimes on paper) with his men to supply them with wages and benefits in return for their services as soldiers.[3] His men were his employees, who could find other jobs if they were unhappy, and therefore had to be treated reasonably well. The contractual relationship was most clear-cut in small units, where the relationship between employer and employees was direct. In larger units a variant form emerged: men were no longer direct employees of the senior commander, but his capital, his major asset which had to be husbanded against loss, since loss of capital would mean loss of power.[4]

Husbanding capital meant treating soldiers decently, paying them well and regularly, caring for their families, and giving them secure employment by doing well at the warlord game. The employer–employee relationship was varnished with a patina of paternalism, the kindly but stern father commanding his loyal and respectful sons. This was the relationship which Feng Yuxiang cultivated with his men; he was their commander, but also their fatherly superior.[5] (It worked well when the officer had age and seniority on his side; it looked rather incongruous when the officer was someone like the sixteen-year old Liu Ruming, who claimed to treat his men with a 'parental attitude'.[6]) Husbanding capital could be achieved also by letting others pay the price of soldiers' contentment, by giving men free reign to exploit the civilian world so long as they were obedient on duty. Many employers less scrupulous than Feng took this path.

In the contractual relationship, soldiers were valuable to their commanders; in other patterns of relationship, they were not. There were enough potential recruits around in warlord China to make it possible to view one's soldiers as disposable. Commanders who saw their men in this way treated them with *indifference and neglect*, as anonymous numbers. The number of men was what counted, not their quality or loyalty. Obedience was secured by harsh discipline, and little attention was given to training or welfare. Soldiers could desert or die, and the commander would simply replace them by new recruitment. There was no real relationship in this, only a temporary crossing of paths. It was characteristic of many of the petty warlord armies, men whose fortunes rose and fell according to the size of their armies. Their fortunes fell because they found it difficult to hang on to their men, and then rose again when they found new suckers willing to enlist.

A second pattern of officer–men relations in which no personal value was assigned to soldiers was the *predatory relationship*, especially characteristic of the lower echelons of officers. Subordinate officers acted concurrently as paymasters; they received funds to pay their men from a higher source. Their men were faceless numbers whose existence could be a source of financial gain. The officer saw the payroll as a means to enrich himself; he retained as large a part of it as he dared. One of Cai Tingkai's commanders kept enough of his men's pay to build himself a western-style villa, in which he maintained a wife and six concubines.[7] Sometimes the predation hurt only the higher command, since the soldiers existed only on paper; otherwise it was a form of embezzlement from the men. It could involve skimming indirect profits, by deducting inflated amounts of money for food and maintenance, as well as direct withholding of wages.

The predatory relationship signified contempt for soldiers; its reward was usually incompetent soldiers. It was a key contributor to the poor quality of warlord troops, and of Guomindang armies after the Northern Expedition. Soldiers were not as stupid as their predatory officers thought. And they felt minimal loyalty or respect for those who traduced them.

One practical way to cement troop loyalty, and to avoid the negative consequences of contractual, negligent or predatory relationships, all of which were impersonal, was to build a force on the basis of existing ties, especially regional ones. We saw above how officers used *regional ties* for recruitment (p. 25). They were the continuing cement of many provincial armies, the ties that an officer used to bind his men to him.[8]

Whatever method a commander chose to handle his troops, none of them implied closeness between officers and men. This was a reflection in part of the gap in social origins between the two. In the late Qing and early Republic the gap in social origins was not great. Until the modern military schools were established, a military career was not attractive. Young men from marginal social and economic backgrounds were drawn into the officer corps, as well as young men who had been displaced from traditional career patterns by the end of the examination system.[9] As the military schools became entrenched, the origins of cadets shifted upwards, especially at top-flight schools such as Baoding and Huangpu, and at foreign military academies. The rise in social origins, and the improvement in officer training, started in the early Republic and accelerated under the Guomindang, contributed to a rise in the social status of the military – but of officers only.[10]

As the shift upwards in social origins gained ground, so the alternative form of officer recruitment, promotion from the ranks, sank into decline. In mainline armies, promotion from the ranks was never a major form of officer selection. In the late Qing Newly Created Army only six of sixty-eight officers had had no military education, a standard indicator of promotion from the ranks.[11] Some very famous warlords did rise from the ranks – Zhang Zuolin, Feng Yuxiang, Zhang Zongchang; these commanders often pulled their former subordinates into the officer corps with them.[12] Cai Tingkai, the leading popular hero in the Guomindang armies, rose from the ranks, as did numbers of senior Red Army officers. But the fame of those who did obscured their small number.

Officers promoted from the ranks tended not to rise very far. In Li Zongren's tiny (3,000 men) first independent command, the senior and middle-ranking officers had attended military school; men promoted from the ranks stuck at the level of lieutenant.[13] A similar pattern shows up in a register of Guangzhou officers, serving and retired, compiled in 1947–8. The survey lists about 2,500 officers, all but 330 of whom were products of military schools. Two hundred and sixty of the 330 never rose above the rank of lieutenant, while only 15 rose to the rank of colonel or above. Most of those who had been promoted from the ranks were already retired in 1947, indicating that movement upwards from the ranks became more difficult over time.[14]

The divergence in social origins was matched by an aloof, elitist caste of mind in the officers, which mirrored the civilian view of soldiers as sordid, stupid creatures. The superior cast of mind was reflected in the elaborate uniforms which officers wore – in contrast to their rumpled men, clad in poor-quality grey cotton uniforms. In the civilian world the gorgeousness of mandarin robes gave way to sober blue gowns or stiff western suits; in the military world the vivid

Qing uniforms were replaced by an eclectic range of the more flamboyant western uniforms, just at the point when western officers were getting out of bright colours and into khaki. (None of the borrowers seemed aware that the most beautiful uniforms were worn by the officers of the worst armies, notably the Russian.) Elaborateness of outfit reached its pinnacle with peacocks such as Zhang Zuolin, usually so laden down with gold braid, medals and cockades that his meagre frame was almost invisible. Lesser officers loved adornment too. The soldiers of one north-west unit described their officers (in 1927) as 'three golds and five leathers' (*sanjin wupi*): gold-rimmed glasses, gold rings and gold watches; leather belts, pouches, boots, batons and gloves.[15]

Not all officers were fashion plates. Feng Yuxiang was famous for his farm-boy outfits, though his wardrobe also contained medal-laden tunics and plumed headgear. Feng had a magnificent physique, and could afford to dress down as well as up. Less well-endowed officers relied on their splendid costumes to set them apart from their scruffy troops. The only really striking soldiers in China, in terms of appearance, were those who served outside the Great Wall: 'In Manchuria and on the Mongol frontier all ranks are supplied with fur caps and long coats lined with sheepskin, but inside the Great Wall the use of furs by soldiers is traditionally effeminate.'[16] Most Chinese soldiers wore drab, cheap grey cotton.

Officers kept away from their men in the normal course of army life. There was little direct contact in barracks or camp. On the march officers were either carried in sedan chairs or rode on horseback. Li Zongren, who resisted the normal pattern of officer hauteur, caused a commotion in the narrow streets of Changsha (Hunan) just after its occupation by Guomindang troops in 1926. Li, marching on foot with his men, ran into an officer of the 8th Army who was being carried in a sedan chair. The officer was junior in rank to Li, and was caught in a high-level etiquette trap; he had to make way for Li, but he could not get his chair out of the way.[17]

The cultivation of the common touch (*pingminhua*) which officers such as Li and Feng practised enhanced their reputations as soldiers (especially with their own men and with foreigners), but it was not widely imitated. The social distance between officers and men widened as the status of the officer corps rose, while that of soldiers remained stationary at a low level. As the distance grew, so the obeisance that officers demanded of their men intensified. By 1948, regulations on when and where Guomindang soldiers should salute their officers covered seven pages, and listed fifty-two separate instances on which a salute was required.[18]

Social distance between officers and men encouraged the maltreatment of soldiers. Maltreatment does not include the routine harshness or the standard Spartan quality of military life. The dividing-line between discipline and maltreatment was crossed when officers treated their men with unnecessary severity, when they paid no attention to their welfare, and when they expected fear rather than respect from their men.

MALTREATMENT

In warlord armies, as in most armies, the decisions on how to treat soldiers were internal ones; officers had the right to abuse or punish soldiers, so long as their superiors permitted it. The army was not subject to civil law. The general assumption was that soldiers had to be treated roughly, to toughen them up for fighting. If they got used to rough handling from their officers, they would find it easier to face the enemy. Frederick the Great's maxim that 'the common soldier must fear his officer more than the enemy' was widely observed.

The most overt forms of maltreatment were physical, either slappings, proddings or beatings by the officers themselves, or beatings administered at their orders. Shen Congwen described the constant slaps and punches which officers administered to recruits as a deliberate way to knock them into shape.[19] That was in the 1910s. Twenty years later one of the first questions in a question-and-answer manual for Guomindang recruits was:

Q. Why do our officers swear at us and punish us?
A. Officers are the fathers and older brothers of soldiers. They must keep discipline, as in a family. They love and care for their men, but they must be strict, otherwise the men will never learn.[20]

The only discipline that these child-like soldiers were thought to understand was beating; casual thumps and deliberate flogging. Xiao Jun's story 'In the army' (see appendix 4) tells in revolting detail of a punishment in which a soldier was given 600 strokes, supervised by the officer but administered by his colleagues.[21] Such ferocious beatings were commonplace. Since the beatings were public and were carried out by other soldiers, the men became accomplices to each others' abuse. The episode of army life that most horrified Warrior (the idealistic young man who enlisted to fight the Japanese in 1934) was seeing his comrades cheerfully beat another recruit senseless, twenty men with canes all pitching in together.[22] Some commanders realised that beatings might produce temporary subservience, but in the long run could only produce resentment. Feng Yuxiang regarded unnecessary beating as counter-productive, and in 1913 issued a set of eight instances in which beating was not permitted (*ba buda*). Officers were forbidden to beat their men in the following circumstances:

- when they themselves had lost their temper
- when the men had been on duty over-time
- when the men were new recruits
- when the men were sick
- when the men were first offenders
- when the weather was excessively cold or hot
- when rations were short
- when a soldier was in a state of grief or misery.[23]

These prohibitions still left plenty of instances in which soldiers could legitimately be beaten, but Feng's subordinate officers were furious, convinced that the men would become truculent and unmanageable. Only the slowing of the desertion rate mollified them.[24]

Beating was usually enough to keep soldiers in line on duty; what they did off duty seldom concerned their officers. If it was not enough, there were severer punishments, ranging from imprisonment to branding to execution. Zhang Zuolin executed 82 men of a regiment which mutinied against him near Haerbin in 1922, and sent the rest of the 700 men back to their native Shandong with brandmarks on their chests to prevent them from ever re-enlisting.[25] This kind of punishment was often designed *pour encourager les autres*, to remind soldiers of what happened to the disobedient. Li Zongren ordered the summary execution of a soldier caught looting in 1920 because 'I suddenly decided to punish severely one or two soldiers as an example to those who had violated military discipline.' Li was unmoved by the fact that all the man had stolen was a bundle of clothes, or that he came from the same county as Li. He had to die because he had disobeyed orders, and the orders had to be seen to have force.[26] Maltreatment should not be regarded as simply a means of maintaining discipline. China's armies had their share of sadistic officers, for whom violence against soldiers was a source of direct pleasure. Officer candidates were not screened for psychological peculiarities at the time, in China or anywhere else, but there is no doubt that many young men attracted to military careers are motivated less by patriotism or a sense of duty, by material or social ambition, than by a deep-seated psychological need. Those who lack self-control may seek a place where violent behaviour is tolerated; those who suffer from anxiety find a highly structured society consoling; those with weak egos are buoyed up by uniform and ritual forms of respect, such as saluting; those with sexual anxieties (especially castration anxiety) may be relieved by wearing a sword or gun.[27]

These categories of officer personality, largely speculative, were devised by an English psychologist, Norman Dixon, as part of an effort to define military incompetence. They were hard to quantify in the English case, and impossible in the Chinese, since no examinations were ever made; no-one at the time ever discussed castration anxiety with Chinese officers. But the idea of the officer who bullies and shouts to compensate for deep inadequacies and anxieties, and who went into the army just so that he could find a way of coping with them, is so persuasive an idea that it may not even need dressing up with theory.

NEGLECT

Beyond obvious maltreatment such as beating were the indirect forms of maltreatment – neglect of soldiers' physical welfare which amounted to passive physical abuse. Officers paid little attention to living conditions. Some soldiers lived in custom-built barracks, others in commandeered temples, schools or public buildings, others in tents. The quarters tended to be dirty, overcrowded and bug-infested, not unusual conditions for men from peasant homes, but still breeding-grounds for infectious diseases. Scabies, eye infections, stomach infections and food poisoning were some of the standard army afflictions. Boils, ringworm, eczema, parasite infestation, venereal diseases and various fevers (yellow, trench, relapsing and sand-fly) were common.[28] More serious were acute illnesses like dysentery and cholera, which cut a swathe through the armies of Zhejiang and Jiangsu in 1924.[29] Disease was a greater danger to soldiers than death or injury in battle, even at times of all-out war. An official account of conditions in Hunan for the years 1938–41 showed that soldiers were six times as likely to fall ill as to be wounded.[30]

In organised communities such as army units it should have been easier to impose sanitation than it would in fragmented civilian society. Lack of sanitation was the major cause of disease and ill health. But few officers bothered with their men's health. The Guomindang army authorities did publish detailed instructions on latrine construction and location – five per hundred men were required, except on the march, when three were sufficient.[31] Feng Yuxiang forced his men to clean their barracks, to wash themselves and to use latrines. He would not permit them to relieve themselves all over railway stations when they were travelling by train, in the usual soldier way. Instead he had troop trains stopped in the countryside, and ordered soldiers to excrete directly on to the fields, where their leavings were useful rather than simply noisome.[32]

Officers' neglect of their soldiers in normal times was compounded in times of fighting. Those who died were spared the ultimate form of callous neglect, the lack of medical care. Most armies made almost no provisions for medical care. A journalist passing through a small village in Pingwu (Sichuan) in 1936 saw the refuse of an army which had preceded him: 'There were about a hundred households there ... and in most of them there were sick soldiers, without clothing, food, medicine, sleeping mats. Most were lying on the mud floors, soaked in urine, filthy beyond belief.'[33] These were men from North China, hundreds of miles away. Their army had deserted them, they had no families there to care for them. They were hours or days away from their deaths. An army on the march discarded sick soldiers; the thought of giving them care, or at least of leaving money to support them, did not arise. The punishment for being wounded, or for falling ill, was a lonely death.

In the Anti-Japanese War the medical service was still the 'stepchild' of the army, under-staffed, under-equipped and viewed by army command as an unnecessary luxury.[34] Fortunate soldiers might get treatment in a mission hospital, but they were scarce, and soldiers were not their favourite patients, unless a mutually satisfactory arrangement could be reached between the mission and the army, as was the case in Huaijing (Henan). There the local commander made one of the Canadian missionary doctors an honorary medical officer, and contributed to the financing of the hospital, which in turn cared for wounded soldiers.[35]

The worst examples of officers' callousness towards their men came from the Anti-Japanese War. The casual maltreatment of soldiers, especially conscripts, shocked foreign reporters, who wrote bitter indictments of the Guomindang army command.[36] By then some of the old patterns of officer–men relations had withered away; the contractual relationship went into abeyance at least in the Guomindang as officer professionalism gained way, transfers of officers from unit to unit became routine, and personal command unusual. Strong regional ties between officers and men were suspect, as the enforced side-lining of some of China's most talented generals, Zhang Fakui, Cai Tingkai and Li Zongren, all of whom had strong armies based on regional ties, underlined. With the withering away of these two patterns of relationship, the negligent and the predatory relationships came to the fore.[37]

The maltreatment of soldiers was an implicit expression of officers' contempt for their men. Few officers noted that there was a correlation between contented soldiers and military success, though the examples of Feng Yuxiang and of the 4th and 7th Armies on the Northern Expedition should have proved beyond doubt that officers who treated their men well got good results out of them. Most saw that soldiers were easily replaceable; they regarded them as stupid, only able to respond to harsh treatment. In the officers' eyes, as in those of civilians, soldiers were the scum of the earth.

5

BANDIT/SOLDIER – SOLDIER/BANDIT

In the turbulent last years of the Qing dynasty, a poor but ambitious young man took the only path that seemed to give him a chance at (local) wealth and power; he became a bandit. He did so well that he became a threat to government forces in his area of West Guangxi. The local commander decided to deal with him by taking him into the army; he became a soldier. In the army he did even better; by 1912 he ruled the whole province. In the next decade he extended his power to Guangdong. In 1921 he was brought down by Cantonese forces, and his power in Guangxi was fragmented into a collection of autonomous units (*zizhijun*), most of which refused his authority. The ageing general called all his enemies bandits – Yuefei (Cantonese bandits), Shenfei (Shen Hongying), Lifei (Li Zongren).[1]

Lu Rongting, the bandit-turned-soldier, labelled as 'bandits' any other soldiers who opposed him. There was no irony intended. He was making a distinction between legitimate soldiers, sanctioned by a higher authority (his own) and illegitimate bandits, men who rejected his authority. The distinction was not his private idiosyncrasy. In the political vacuum that followed the end of the Qing, legitimacy came to be defined principally in military terms; men who had military power conferred legitimacy on themselves and their followers. They called themselves generals, and their enemies bandits. In the process they seemed to make the distinction between soldiers and bandits meaningless.

For civilians there was no semantic problem; they knew the distinction had gone, and that soldiers and bandits were indistinguishable (*bingfei bufen*). They called soldiers 'official bandits' (*guanfei*). They knew it as the victims of armed men; it made little difference whether their oppressors were legitimate or illegitimate.

There were distinctions to be made, though not in terms of name-calling or of being victimised. The distinctions become apparent if we move away from the generalised term of abuse *fei*, and use the more precise term *tufei*, 'local bandits'. Soldiers belonged to formal, complex organisations, armies; bandits belonged to loose organisations, gangs. Armies overtly controlled specific areas, collected taxes and gave orders to officials; bandits might be strong enough to control an area, but they did it covertly. Soldiers were stationed in towns, along roads and railways; bandits lived in hills, marshes and wildernesses. Soldiers were mobile, could be transferred from one place to another; bandits stayed in their own locality. Soldiers wore uniforms; bandits did not. Soldiers' misdeeds were looting, requisitioning, tax-squeezing and press-ganging of coolies; bandits went in for robbery, kidnapping and protection rackets. The rich feared bandits, who could hold them to ransom; the poor feared soldiers, who could bled them dry.[2] The bandits were hit-and-run artists, the coarse comb; the soldiers were systematic plunderers, the fine comb.[3]

These distinctions were real, but they were fully true only of either end of a continuum. At one end were soldiers of well-organised armies, who bore little likeness to bandits; at the other were old-style bandits who had no resemblance to the military. In the extensive middle, the two worlds of bandits and of soldiers overlapped. In this overlapping zone distinctions were blurred, relations were close, behaviour was very similar and there was a recurring two-way traffic – soldiers becoming bandits and bandits becoming soldiers. In the dead centre, the two worlds were united. In the Nanyang region of southern Henan, separate worlds existed in name but not in fact. Between soldiers, bandits and officials there was a stable pattern of mutual aid and cooperation, in which the bandits actually had the upper hand.[4]

Southern Henan was one of the areas of China in which banditry was most rampant. Elsewhere the apparent separation between the licit and the illicit was greater. Sometimes there was a tacit demarcation of spheres of activity, the soldiers dominating the towns and the bandits the rural areas. Lingxian (Shandong) was infested with bandits; the local garrison stayed in its barracks in the county town and left the countryside to the bandits.[5] The 300 garrison troops of Chaocheng (Shandong) were outnumbered by 500 bandits; they preferred not to take the field against them, and left them to their own devices.[6] In areas where bandits were strongly entrenched, provinces such as Henan, Shandong and Sichuan, and the hill and marsh regions of many other provinces, it was sensible for a commander to leave the bandits in peace in their own territories, rather than divert his own energies to attacking them.

'Leaving the bandits in peace' included connivance in their activities. Bandits who were also smugglers needed the military to turn a blind eye to their trade; this could be arranged, for a fee or for a cut of the profits, by discreet payments to local officers.[7] Mutual hands-off arrangements were satisfactory to both sides, so long as neither interfered in the other's activities. These types of informal arrangements hurt only the civilian population, who were ensured a miserable stability of exploitation.

The situations described above suggest a near equality between soldiers and bandits, in terms of local power. In one respect bandits were clearly dependent on soldiers, namely in the supply of arms and ammunition. Soldiers had access to Chinese and foreign sources of arms, from arsenals and from the dubious characters who peddled arms to large-scale consumers – the armies.[8] Bandits could get arms from non-military sources, by purchase, by theft or as part of ransom demands, but none of these sources was reliable, especially in terms of getting weapons with matching ammunition. For that the army was the best source. In some places bandits could buy arms directly from the army. In Shuyang (Jiangsu) the local garrison sold the local bandits whatever they wanted. Shuyang's bandits were described by one angry commentator as the henchmen of the military in fleecing the poor:

If you go into the reasons for Shuyang's fame as an area which produces bandits, you will find that it has nothing to do with Shuyang having so many poor people. Really it is caused by the local military selling guns and bullets to the bandits, working hand in glove with them to go and rob the ordinary people. That's the game the local military is good at.[9]

Sometimes the basis of supply was rental rather than purchase. The militia chief of Mianzhou (Sichuan) rented his rifles to local bandits for one *yuan* a night, plus a share of any profit from activities they were used in; he had them back for militia use during the day.[10] Sometimes bandits got their weapons from the army for free, by enlisting for a while and then defecting with their army-issue guns. The Henan bandit Lao Yangren ('The Foreigner', named for his pale complexion) got 80,000 rifles by enlisting with his numerous followers for a brief stint in Wu Peifu's army.[11] Arms could also be acquired from battlefields, from defeated soldiers and from raids on arsenals. The army was ubiquitous, and bandits had little difficulty arming themselves.

The direct and indirect ways in which the army aided or tolerated bandits exacted a great cost from civilians, who were powerless before both. It was hard to tell which group they would rather do without. When Yan Xishan started his campaign against Nanjing in 1930, he withdrew most of his garrison troops from northern Hubei. Bandit activity surged up as soon as the soldiers were gone.[12] But if soldiers came into an area to suppress bandits, the local population had to thank their saviours with payments in cash, in kind and in labour.[13] Neither situation was the least bit desirable, which is why civilians so often refused to make any distinction between soldiers and bandits, and called them *alter egos* (*huashen*).[14] (See appendix 5.)

In terms of origin, they often were *alter egos*. Bandit activity was most rampant in the hilly, poverty-stricken regions which produced the greatest numbers of soldiers – southern Henan, northern Jiangsu, western Guangxi, western Hunan, and much of Sichuan and Manchuria. In these wretched regions (excluding Manchuria, which was more like the Wild West), recruits to the legal military world and to the illegal bandit world came from the same backgrounds. Young men who left their homes because they were displaced by poverty, because they were in trouble at home or because they wanted some adventure went either to the army or to a bandit gang. Theoretically they became either soldiers or bandits; in actuality they became armed men who could serve in either capacity. Whether an individual kept to one role depended less on his own inclination than on external exigencies, the chief of which, for those whose first role was that of bandit, was the army's need for recruits.

Armies recruited bandits for pragmatic reasons. Bandits came with ready-made qualifications as fighters. They were already on 'active service', and this made them especially useful for emergency recruitment. The pattern was set immediately after the 1911 Revolution. Early in 1912, about 70,000 bandits were recruited into the armies of the Republic in Guangdong; the military situation was so critical that there was no time to discriminate.[15] To disguise their origins, they were known as 'irregulars' (*minjun*). In 1918, when Sun Yat-sen's supporters were scrambling to get men for the (abortive)

Northern Expedition from Guangdong, recruiters combed bandit lairs in Guangxi for new recruits:[16] 'Recruiters visited the robber groups at their various rendezvous in the mountain fastnesses of the province.' The bandits were promised pardons, a share of the campaign spoils and (for the leaders) army commissions. Bandit gangs were the *de facto* military reserves in numbers of regions. In Shanxi (1916) the chief distinction between soldiers and bandits was that soldiers were on the official army payrolls and bandits were not. Soldiers cost the provincial authorities direct cash payments; bandits cost the local populations.[17]

Recruiting bandits as soldiers (*yu bing yu fei*) cut short the laborious process of recruiting and training individual civilians. Bandits knew how to handle weapons, how to live off the land. Another advantage was that they could be brought into the army in groups, with their own existing structure of command and coordination. Bandit recruitment in groups was attractive to ambitious subordinate commanders who wanted to go out on their own. They could rapidly put together something that looked like the army, as the former schoolteacher Liu Zhenhua did in 1912, when he made up an army out of Henanese bandits in a few weeks.[18] This model was a major route for subordinates betraying their commanders; until the moment of betrayal it was difficult to use regular recruiting channels, but clandestine arrangements could be made with bandits.

Recruiting bandits could also be used to fulfil one of the main formal tasks of garrison forces, the eradication of banditry. If bandits became soldiers, they were no longer bandits. Recruiting them was quicker, cheaper, safer and smoother than fighting them. In Shaoxing (Zhejiang) a local bandit gang was 'eradicated' in this way in 1923, though without the chief, who was executed.[19] In Henan (1922–3) a regional bandit suppression commissioner, appointed in November, was able to report complete success by January. His success came from the fact that he had enlisted 4,000 bandits into the local army.[20]

Pacification of bandits by incorporating them into the army did not start with the warlord period. We have already seen that this was the route by which Lu Rongting joined the army. Cen Chunxuan, the viceroy of Guangdong and Guangxi in the last years of the Qing, dealt with Guangxi's overwhelming bandit problem by taking a portion of them into the army.[21] The prefect of Ximin (Liaoning) got together an effective garrison by recruiting a local bandit, Zhang Zuolin, making him garrison commander, and getting him to bring along 230 of his bandit comrades as garrison troops.[22] Former bandits were especially effective as bandit suppression agents, since they knew how to flush out their former colleagues and adversaries from the bandit world. Lu Rongting kept banditry in control in Guangxi for more than a decade; the ex-bandit was a formidable bandit-eradicator.[23] In 1924, the magistrate of Linqu (Shandong) chose the same tactic to deal with the county's bandit problem. His first appointee was a failure, but the second bandit he appointed to head a special bandit suppression unit did the job.[24]

Bandit incorporation solved immediate bandit problems, and also kept temporarily quiescent but potentially troublesome men out of the way. Many of the followers of the White Wolf (North China's most flamboyant bandit) were taken into the regular army after his defeat and death, to prevent them from organising in his name again.[25] Bandits in the army were less likely to cause trouble than ex-bandits floating loose, for the army offered them levels of comfort and security which were difficult to duplicate in bandit life.

Bandits found the army a congenial livelihood. Soldiering was a variant form of their bandit life, but one with greater potential. Lu Rongting and his men found the army safer than banditry, and more gratifying to the ego. There were opportunities for self-aggrandisement, in the form of titles and uniforms, which were not appropriate for bandits. To acquire what amounted to an elevation in social status, their actual behaviour did not have to change – 'the greenwood became the Green Standard' (*lulin bian xiang luying*).[26] A bandit whose livelihood was insecure, who was competing with other bandits or being harassed enough by local authorities to make his life uncomfortable, would gravitate towards the local army:[27] 'The type of man who is most likely to join the army is the pirate or robber who is beginning to find things too hot for him, or that there are too many on the job.' This was an observation from Guandong, in 1912. It underlines the fact that banditry could be a very insecure mode of life, especially in contrast to that of soldiers.

One of the aspects in which soldiers' lives were easier than bandits' was material gain. Soldiers could loot on a grander, more systematic scale than bandits. They were legitimate, and did not have to creep around at night. They were under no constraint to stay on reasonable terms with their immediate neighbours in the civilian world, as bandits were: 'the rabbit does not eat the grass at the rim of his burrow'. The bandits recruited in Guangxi in 1918 were impressed with the rewards of soldiering:[28] 'The fighting in Hunan, where pillage and plunder were carried out wholesale, offered greater opportunity for speedy enrichment with less liability to danger, than did their former lawless occupations in the old Guangxi haunts.'

Some bandits had ambitions beyond enrichment in the army; they wanted a military career. By working themselves up in the outlaw world, they could acquire enough men and enough local nuisance value to enable them to transfer laterally into the army, avoiding the slow process of rising through the ranks. This was the ambition of a Sichuan bandit, just before the 1911 Revolution:

He wanted to become a great man, a colonel, and with this end in view, had recently joined a group of bandits operating in the vicinity. For this calling he was well suited, being quick, skillful and merciless. He knew that after a few successfully perpetrated robberies and kidnappings, accounts of his boldness and bravery would reach the government of Teh Chien. Then a man would be sent to negotiate with him, to suggest that he and his followers take service with the taoyin of Teh Chien. He might be made the leader of a battalion or a regiment.[29]

Some bandits were so keen to get into the army that they did not wait for recruiters to come to them, but forced the army's hand, usually by kidnapping a prominent person. In March 1918, two American engineers were kidnapped in Henan. The bandit terms for their release were (1) a supply of arms and ammunition; (2) the incorporation of 2,000 bandits into the local army; and (3) the appointment of the bandit chief as a captain in the army. The first two demands were rejected by negotiators, but the third was accepted by the local army commander and was enough to get the captives released.[30]

The most famous episode of importunate incorporation into the army was the 'Lincheng Outrage' of 1923. About 1,200 bandits, most of them former soldiers of Zhang Jingyao, held up the Blue Train near Lincheng (Shandong), and took a large number of hostages, Chinese and foreign. One of the foreigners was Miss Aldrich, sister-in-law of John D. Rockefeller, whose capture ensured massive publicity. Another was J. B. Powell, editor of the *China Weekly Review*, who provided the reports on which the publicity was based, direct from the bandits' lair. This was an early hijacking, and though it happened before the days of television coverage, the fame of the captives (Miss Aldrich was actually soon released) and the fortuitous capture of a journalist made it a media event, inside China and beyond.

The main negotiating demand of the bandits was for incorporation into the army, for themselves and for 10,500 other local bandits. They wanted to be organised into four brigades, each fully armed, with six months' pay in advance.[31] Sun Meiyao, their leader, presented their demands in the form of a statement of grievance:

This is to notify the facts that we have hitherto been law-abiding citizens and that we have no desire to become robbers, but in this troubled era of unreliable government we find ourselves compelled to take risks in order to obtain redress for our grievances.

The militarist party has treated us badly. At the time when Chang Ching-yao, the former military governor, recruited us, we rejoiced exceedingly, hoping we would be useful to our country. On the fall of Chang Ching-yao we were immediately disbanded; this was held to be an injustice. We returned to our homes from Hunan and took up peaceful work, but evil minded landowners falsely accused us of being bandits. This rendered it impossible for us to remain in the homes we possessed, and we have no place left to us. All of us therefore who are in this plight have gathered together and have occupied the hill of Pao Tzu-ku as our base. Suddenly the 20th Brigade arrived and demanded surrender of ourselves and of our arms. We would willingly have surrendered but we feared injustice. We therefore looted the train on the 21st day of the third moon. We have no desire to rob the articles which we took, but we know that foreigners are to be relied upon, while our government departments and troops are absolutely unreliable. There is no alternative.[32]

Sun was right about the influence of foreigners. Their presence as hostages forced the local authorities to resolve the situation by acceding to the bandits' demands. Their grievances were not redressed in full, but Sun came down from the mountain as a brigadier, and took command at the army headquarters from which operations against him had been directed.[33]

Given the willingness of bandits to go into the army, and the ease with which they could be recruited, few commanders ignored this source of soldiers. Even the Red Army recruited bandits in its early days in Jinggangshan. Those who did refuse had practical reasons. Huang Shaoxiong complained that his refusal to recruit Guangxi bandits in the early 1920s put him at a disadvantage *vis-à-vis* his rivals in the petty warlord game.[34] But his refusal was the sacrifice of short-term advantage for long-term gain. He saw the drawbacks of recruiting bandits. Armies got men who were tough, aggressive fighters, but they also got liabilities. Bandits took discipline poorly, they were restless and hard to please. If the army did not meet their expectations, they would leave for the hills again; their arms and ammunition would go with them. A commander who wanted to build up a solid, reliable force as the basis for his own expansionist ambitions, as Huang did, would spurn bandits and go after raw young men.

In the units which did recruit them, bandits were not trusted. Their commanders recognised them for what they were, men one step away from outlawry; there was no guarantee that they would not get from the army the punishment that the law had impotently threatened them with as bandits. This is what happened to Sun Meiyao. His time in favour lasted only six months. Then he was arrested, charged with having kept weapons confiscated from other bandits for his own use, and executed, to shrieks of *Schadenfreude*.[35] Lao Yangren met the same kind of end. He allowed himself and his men to be taken into Wu Peifu's armies in 1922, to save Wu the trouble of suppressing him. But Wu changed the terms of their agreement, and tried to transfer the bandit and his men to Sichuan. They deserted, back to the bandit world. His men were sorry to leave, and they now betrayed their chief, killing him and using his severed head as their re-entry permit to the army.[36] He had outsmarted himself, forgetting a cardinal rule: in the end the army had the upper hand. However thin the distinction between the army and the bandit worlds, the legal forces had the edge over the illegal ones.

The relative superiority of the soldier world was borne out by the fact that moving the other way, from the army into the bandit world, was less a question of choice than of necessity. Becoming a bandit was one of two not very desirable choices for soldiers who had been disgraced, defeated, demobilised or driven to desert. The other choice was going back to civilian life, not a happy prospect for men who had been a long time away from the rigours of farm work, owned no land and had no marketable skill.

Chinese armies were major sources of bandits. Civilians were driven into banditry in a number of fairly haphazard ways. Some were driven in by poverty, or by the impact of a natural disaster; others went in because bandit life suited their personalities. A few were born into bandit families. The armies of warlord China actually produced bandits, since the leavings of the military world were likely to look to the outlaw world to make their living.

Defeated soldiers were one of the largest categories of soldier recruits to banditry. With defeat they lost their unit, their source of income and their commander. With luck they retained their weapons, their passport to a career in banditry. These 'scattered soldiers' (*sanbing*) had seen their rice bowl cracked. If they could not find another regular army unit to take them on, banditry offered the nearest approximation to their accustomed life-style.

Demobilised soldiers were less likely to turn to banditry, so long as their demobilisation was properly handled and their way back to civilian life made smooth by the payment of a bonus, by the arrangement for travel back to their native place, and by the provision of some form of employment. If none of these steps were taken, they were almost forced to turn to banditry. Here was the creation of a vicious circle. Those commanders who though of mass demobilisation as the means to reduce China's burden of soldiers were well aware of the bandit alternative. This was one of the reasons why demobilisation plans so often remained on paper (see chapter 8).

The disgraced soldier was in a different situation. He had got into trouble in the army, and for him banditry was a safe haven from punishment. Being a bandit was less secure than being in the army, but was an improvement over being dead or in prison. Deserters also looked to banditry as a haven; unless they could slip back easily into civilian life, it was the only way out for them.

The transition from army to banditry was not easy; new bandits either had to attach themselves to an existing band or compete with established bandits, especially tricky in bandit-ridden areas. Bandit life was more precarious. The risk of death in battle was diminished, the heavy hand of discipline was gone, but so was the supply of food, money, arms and ammunition. Soldier entrants to banditry saw it as a second-best form of armed life, a painful necessity rather than a desired life-style. But those who lost their place in the army, especially after a long period of service, were 'dogs without a home' (*sangjia zhi gou*), faced with a choice between destitution and the lawless world.[37]

For a soldier to leave the army and become a bandit was a step down in the hierarchy of armed men. For the civilian world it was often a calamity. The great fear of localities which saw armies defeated or disbanded in their neighbourhood was that there would be a sudden rise in the number of local bandits. Localities could protect themselves by raising militias to push the potential bandits out, as Hexian (Guangxi) did in 1927, when a special militia unit was raised to chase off the defeated soldiers of Shen Hongying, ex-bandit soldiers now returning to banditry.[38] Other localities were not so fortunate, unless so saturated with bandits that there was no room for further competition. In such cases the new entrant might be forced to move far afield to take up his new calling. Sun Meiyao and his men moved from Hunan to Shandong, hundreds of miles across country, to establish their own bandit lair. H. Howard, an American kidnapped by bandits in northern Manchuria (1925), was astonished to find among his captors former soldiers and even officers from all over China who had moved to Manchuria to be bandits, the underbelly of the mass migration into Manchuria taking place at the time.[39]

In most cases soldiers took to the hills where they left the army, and stayed there until they could get back into the army, unless they found being a bandit preferable, in which case their conversion to banditry was final. So long as banditry was a palatable option to ex-soldiers, there was no possibility of eradicating bandits. The visible effects of banditry did decline slowly. The early 1920s, especially in the hills and marshes of North China, were the heyday of banditry and bandits were less rampant during the period of Guomindang control which followed. That did not mean they had ceased to exist.

The soldier and bandit worlds did not always coexist. Some armies did prosecute bandits, some refused to recruit men of bandit origin. Some bandits did cut their ties with the outlaw world permanently after enlistment, especially if a political conversion was involved. He Long is the most famous example. He became a sincere communist, and only used his bandit connections for the benefit of the Red Army. But these instances were not enough to reduce the validity of the general perception of an indivisible armed world. Banditry flourished side by side with the flourishing armies. Civilians had to watch in impotence as bandits went into the army and soldiers turned to banditry. The routine exploitation of the unarmed was no easier to bear because it was routine; it simply came as less of a shock, as one would be less shocked to be mugged in New York than in Toronto. The saying 'soldiers and bandits are indistinguishable' was not a phlegmatic, detached observation but a cry of pain.

6

GREY RATS AND GREY WOLVES

> The grey rats and grey wolves
> Keep on jumping over our walls,
> Keep on eating our goats,
> Keep on hurting our people,
> Keep on wearing our clothes,
> Keep on smashing our shrines.
> O Heaven, O Earth,
> You tell us where to go.[1]

This plaintive lament came from a Henanese peasant. His tormentors were not landlords or officials, not foreign imperialists, but grey rats and grey wolves – his fellow-peasants in army uniform. The people who made him call despairingly to Heaven and Earth were the lawless soldiers of warlord China.

Traditional China was not a peaceable kingdom. The violence that went with peasant rebellions and even more with their suppression, the feuding between clans, the marauding of bandits, the onslaughts of foreign invaders, all produced horrific violence and blood-letting. But most of these were sporadic forms of violence, furious but short lived and localised. Violence was not endemic to Chinese society, as it was to Russian or Irish society. Violence was a last resort, not a standard or respected practice.

The low level of violence had to do partly with the philosophical and institutional underpinnings of the Chinese state, which were designed to defuse potentially violent situations. The traditional elite preferred to exert its authority through pacific, manipulative means rather than through the direct application of force. There were other, more mundane reasons for the disdain of violence. One was the minor role in Chinese culture of alcohol, the fuel of casual violence in many societies. Another was the lack of popular adulation for brute strength in sports, such as prize-fighting, wrestling or team games; the Chinese forms of sporting activity, especially the martial arts, stressed skill and speed, not raw, crude strength. Traditional China did not outlaw violence, but it did not give it an admired or recognised role.

All that changed with the rise of warlordism. The traditional, sporadic forms of violence continued; clans went on fighting each other, peasants rose periodically in violent protest, and were put down violently by the authorities; bandits flourished. To these traditional forms was added a much more pervasive, continuous form of violence – that of soldiers against civilians. The development of new armed forces meant the infliction of misery and fear on civilians as ex-peasants strutted their way to power over the sufferings of their former brothers. Few parts of China were immune. Traditional peasant rebellions, even such great cataclysms as the Taiping Rebellion, had been localised. Soldier violence was not. Everywhere civilians were at the mercy of soldiers; the old power relationship in which the brush ruled the sword was replaced by one in which the man with the gun dominated the unarmed world.[2]

The possession of a gun, however old and battered, with or without ammunition, gave the soldier power. He could humiliate, terrify and abuse people who would have been immune to him before he became a soldier. He could inflict damage with little fear of punishment, since his commander, if he was typical of warlord commanders, would ignore his behaviour. Many even encouraged their men to take what they wanted from civilians, because it absolved them of the responsibility to pay their men. Yang Ximin, a Yunnan warlord, admonished his unpaid and complaining soldiers when he was in occupation in Guangzhou in 1924: 'Since you have guns, why should you be short of rations?'[3] A commander could make his men brave in battle by dangling before them the prospect of loot. Huang Yexing, a petty warlord in southern Guangdong, urged his reluctant men into battle by yelling at them: 'Get going! If you don't advance, all the loot will be grabbed by the others.'[4] The exceptions, commanders who restrained the rampages of their troops, were few.

The violence which soldiers practised against civilians can be divided into two large categories: that inflicted by the army as an institution, and that inflicted by soldiers as individuals or in groups.

I shall look briefly at the first, which has already been discussed extensively in a number of studies of warlordism,[5] and then in greater detail at the second.

In discussing the effects of soldier violence on the civilian population, I have relied quite heavily on the reports of foreign observers, particularly the missionary stringers of the *North China Herald*. Their vantage point was a special one. They lived in the provinces, and they saw the depredations of soldiers at first hand, but they were immune from them. The only real danger to them was that they might be kidnapped, and held to ransom by bandits or by especially lawless soldiers, a dangerous but seldom life-threatening experience which guaranteed a temporary fame. Their immunity did not make them complacent; on the contrary, it gave them the chance to voice their indignation, which the victims could not. It also enabled them to see the actual effects of soldier violence more clearly than the people who were enmired in it, and demoralised by their impotence. The role of foreign observers in reporting the suffering of others is important wherever they have the freedom and the means to do so. Normally we expect the task to be undertaken by foreign correspondents: in the case of China, by journalists such as Edgar Snow, Theodore White or Agnes Smedley. Here the 'journalists' whose reports I have used were missionaries.

Damages inflicted by the army as an institution included the following: requisitioning of goods; conscription of coolies (*lafu*); destruction of property, through occupation or fighting; disruption of trade and transport. All of these were pervasive phenomena. In 1931–2, not a particularly bad year for military activity, 851 out of 941 counties in China suffered some form or other of military requisitioning of goods and the means of transport.[6] Special taxation was another form of extracting support from civilian populations. It was a standard practice, worse in some places, such as the province of Sichuan, but still universal.[7] These two forms of depredation, referred to as *bingchai*, tended to fall most heavily on the peasant or urban masses since the proceeds were usually collected on behalf of the army by local elites, the local authorities or merchant guilds (*shanghui*). The army stated its demands, the local power-holders filled them; if they collected more in the process than the army had actually asked for, or if they allowed the burden to fall more heavily on others than on themselves, the army was not concerned.[8] Conscription of coolies fell most heavily on poor and ignorant men who were strong enough to be useful but not rich or clever enough to buy themselves out.

Damages inflicted on property were no respecters of rank. Large buildings (schools, temples, government offices) were most likely to be requisitioned for accommodation of soldiers. The damage incurred in actual warfare was quite arbitrary. Any person or building or person in the line of fire was at risk. In April 1917, when Sichuanese troops besieged Yunnanese troops in the old imperial city in the centre of Chengdu, all the inhabitants suffered equally, some when their homes were hit by shells, some when their dwellings were razed to open up a clear field of fire.[9]

No place in China, except the foreign concessions (until the Japanese attack on Shanghai in 1932), was safe from the damage of warfare. In 1930, the holiest of holies, the Confucian Temple in Qufu, was heavily damaged by shelling in a battle between troops of Yan Xishan and the Central Government. Holes were smashed in walls, roofs and ceilings, trees splintered and gravestones shattered. The local gazetteer listed fifty-eight separate areas of damage within the temple compound.[10]

These were the wounds that the army as an institution inflicted on the body of Chinese society. The attacks were impersonal; military men could explain them away as 'inevitable consequences of warfare', as they still do today (as in the Israeli siege of Beirut). The marauding behaviour of soldiers was different; in each of its forms it involved the pursuit of personal gain or pleasure.

LOOTING

Looting was a particular threat to urban residents. Villages were sometimes looted, as were forty-two in Dingxian (Hebei) in 1927, by retreating Fengtian troops; the average loss per household was 2.6 *yuan*; in the worst hit villages the loss rose to 27.3 *yuan*.[11] But few villages had the magnetic attraction for soldier-looters of urban concentrations of wealth. Looting tended to take place at specific times, when a city or town was being evacuated by defeated troops or when victorious troops were taking over a city; when troops mutinied or when their pay was in arrears. Looting was a different form of theft from the legalised theft of requisitioning, or the routine petty theft of soldiers; it was usually concentrated into a brief, wild orgy of noise, shooting, smashing and grabbing.

When a city or town was looted, rich and poor were victims together (see appendix 3). The aim of looting was strictly material. The goods of the poor were easier to grab, but less valuable than the well-protected goods of the rich and of shops. The desire was for material things, but if human beings got in the way of looters, or if walls or furniture stood between looters and their goals, they had to be destroyed. The frenzied lust for the fruits of loot was not a particularly Chinese phenomenon. One of the worst episodes of looting in Chinese history was the explosion of greed, the insatiable rapacity of foreign troops, during the occupation of Beijing after the Boxer Rising in 1900. Looters were simply soldiers released from army discipline who took advantage of the anarchy they created in an unarmed society.

Incidents of looting followed grimly similar lines. The looting of Xuzhou (Jiangsu) in 1912, by mutineers from Zhang Xun's army, was little different from other episodes:

The sun rose this morning on the complete wreck of what yesterday was a splendid town. Every shop worth looting was cleaned out and the whole row of prosperous shops on both sides of the main street outside the South Gate were burned and totally destroyed, for a distance of perhaps two hundred yards. Inside the city there was little burning, but far greater loss of life. In a walk of half a mile. Ten bodies were found . . .

The whole population seemed to go crazy at once. Everybody began to run somewhere else. The shopmen gazed stupidly at the tumult for a second, and then they heard the cry: the rebels have entered the city! I have seen some quick moving at various times in my life, but never anything to beat the speed with which the shops put up their front doors. As I turned the first corner, I heard the second shout: It's the mutiny of Chang's troops! Immediately the rifles began to crack, the bullets to whiz. By the time I reached home and secreted a few valuables, the whole town was in a mad loot. Not only were the shops looted, but every rich man's house was spotted and looted before the people began to realise what was going on. The richest family in the city, the Changs, is only a few steps from the Presbyterian compound, and we had a fine view of all that transpired. For half an hour a steady stream of silks, furs, quilts, cash and even horses and mules poured out . . .

As soon as the Changs were cleaned out, attention was turned to the business section, with the results above stated. By midnight the shops were all done for and for the remaining hours private families of standing were all included in the wreck.[12]

Lootings were cataclysmic, terrifying experiences for their victims. They descended like the whirlwind and blew themselves out only when the troops were satiated. The only defence for civilians was to hide themselves and their possessions, or to seek refuge in foreign compounds which were usually safe from looters.

Some places were looted more often than others. Wealthy cities such as Chengdu were looted repeatedly; strategic centres such as Xuxhou, Loyang or Kaifeng, which changed hands often, suffered regularly. But the occasion rather than the place dictated an outbreak of looting; soldiers looted when they were disgruntled, or when they knew they could get away with it.

Prosperous places could recover from being looted (even without private insurance) but poorer ones could be devastated permanently. A visitor to Fuzhou (Shaanxi) in 1916 found the town virtually abandoned; it had been looted four times in the recent past, and its inhabitants had finally been forced to desert it.[13] The same fate befell the string of small commercial centres along the West River in Guangxi in the early 1920s. First Cantonese troops moved up the river, and looted each town along their path. When they were driven back out of the province, they looted each town again on the way out. The Yunnanese troops who were pursuing them looted on their way down to Guangzhou, and, some time later, on their way back. Finally in 1925 the Guangxi Clique set up a stable administration and restored order. By that time, many of the towns had been so damaged that they had sunk into hopeless apathy and despondency, trade had almost ceased, and only opium continued to flow.[14]

RAPE

Rape was the form of soldier violence which aroused the greatest fear – in women and girls, and in their fathers, husbands and brothers. The fear of rape was certainly more pervasive than the actual incidence, but the fear was based on reality. In a sexually puritan society, rape was such an appalling happening that it could scarcely be mentioned. The victims of rape were defiled, and their families with them.

Again, there was nothing specifically Chinese about soldier rapists, nor about the fear of rape. Soldiers are generally feared as rapists, lustful brutes who are not restrained by the normal social controls which protect women. The fear is associated especially with invading foreign armies; the particularly anguishing aspect of rape in warlord China was that it was not barbarian troops who attacked Chinese women, but Chinese troops. Chinese women could never be completely safe when so many soldiers were on the loose. In a period when the traditional restrictions on women were beginning to give way to more liberal ideas about proper female behaviour, the real danger of rape kept them confined to the care of their male relatives.

Rape was too appalling to describe in detail, or even directly. It was referred to in veiled terms. A missionary in Anqing (Anhui) could only bring himself to imply that ghastly things had happened to a group of girl students in the sericulture school when a band of soldiers burst in.[15] In 1920, Li Zongren tried to get a group of 'scattered troops' away from their female victims, without success. In his account, he could only speak of 'terrible screams' and 'sorrowful moans' and of the 'animal passions' of the soldiers.[16] No descriptions were really necessary, for rape was as awful in the imagining as in stark fact. A rare vivid description by Tian Jun (in *Village in August*) of the rape of a Chinese woman by a Japanese soldier is more graphic but no more chilling that the veiled references.[17]

THEFT

Soldier theft from civilians took many forms. It could mean direct theft, the actual stealing of goods, a chicken for a meal, a warm quilt, clothing, anything that caught the soldier's eye, plus an animal to take away what had been stolen. This kind of theft was a normal, everyday event. It forced people to conceal what they did not want stolen, and to resign themselves to the loss of what they could not protect. There were also indirect forms of theft, in which worthless paper or metal currency was forced on impotent sellers.

Most warlords printed their own paper money, which, since it was usually unbacked, had no real exchange value. They also issued adulterated metal currencies, whose value varied with the degree of debasement. Merchants and other hapless sellers would be forced to accept the money at its face value, often making an involuntary gift of the goods or services being 'sold'. Some of the paper money was of such poor quality that there was barely a pretence of making a sale:[18] 'Complaint is made because of the paper wearing out when it comes into contact with perspiration and of the ink fading, rendering the bill worthless.' This form of theft-through-purchase carried an additional insult when the soldier demanded 'change' for a purchase in real money, using large paper bills to make small purchases and taking the change in sound metal currency.[19]

Another form of indirect theft was the enforced discounting of purchases in all stores in a locality through 'agreement' between the army command and the local merchants' guild. Lao Yangren's men, in one of the periods when they were soldiers rather than bandits, demanded and received an eighty per cent discount on all purchases made in Bozhou (Anhui).[20] Soldiers might also barter with civilians, with goods which the civilians did not necessarily want. Yunnanese troops often used opium as currency, a far less disadvantageous transaction for the purchaser than many others with soldiers, but not good for the health of the community.[21]

Soldiers routinely stole services as well as goods – meals in restaurants, rides in rickshaws, train trips, visits to prostitutes, entertainment. The missionaries of Xiangtan (Hunan) were scandalised when soldiers broke down the doors of the Presbyterian Church Community Guild to get into a weekly film show.[22]

Finally soldiers could steal money by ransoming goods and animals to their owners, a two-stage form of theft in which the item was stolen and then 'sold' back to its owner.[23] This practice could extend to the actual flesh of the individual; one source claimed that in Ganzhou (Jiangxi) men were kidnapped and then sold back to their families by weight, 'thirty cents a catty, just a little dearer than pork'.[24]

Soldiers were licensed thieves, licensed by the guns they carried. It is only in the context of routine theft that the Red Army regulations that soldiers should not steal from the public looked revolutionary at all. (The Red Army could substitute confiscation for theft, depriving the wealthy of their goods to support the cause of the poor.) Soldiers stole from those least able to protect their goods, the poor and people who did business in public places. The possessions of the rich were accessible only in times of looting; otherwise they were securely protected behind walls. As time went on, the rich removed their goods from areas of soldier activity altogether, into the foreign concessions. The rapacity of soldier-thieves was one part of a conglomeration of pressures which pushed the rural elite increasingly into the cities, and into those parts of China outside the range of Chinese soldiers.

VANDALISM AND CASUAL VIOLENCE

Looting and theft satisfied greed; rape satisfied lust. But many of the acts of violence which occurred with sickening regularity through the warlord period were self-fulfilling, manifestations of a love of violence for its own sake, casual, pointless acts of spoiling and destruction. The wreckage that soldiers made of the schools, temples and other public and private buildings where they were billeted was one form of the wantonness of soldiers. Long Jiguang's Guangxi troops reduced the Gongye Xuetang in Guangzhou to rubble during the three months that they stayed there.[25] Sometimes destruction was done in the (spurious) name of collecting firewood, as when soldiers occupying the Confucian Temple in Cangzhou (Hebei) used the memorial tablets enshrined there to fuel their stoves.[26] But usually soldier vandalism was the work of rowdy, uncontrolled young men who liked smashing things up.

They also enjoyed smashing up people. A soldier in Guiyang (Guizhou) kicked a man to death in front of a crowd of civilians because the man had inadvertently bumped into him.[27] A labour conscript in Sichuan who tried to run away was shot to death 'like a dog' right in front of a foreign witness.[28]

Casual violence was used to humiliate and degrade civilians. Soldiers seemed to love seeing people scuttle away from them or cower before them in terror. A young Sichuanese who was billeted on a wealthy Chengdu family in the mid 1920s described with relish how he and his comrades treated the family. They did little actual damage. They got their pleasure from keeping the family in a state of extreme anxiety. They kicked over dining tables, grabbed food from people's bowls, made lewd remarks to the women, gave threatening gestures. They had the time of their lives in scaring their unwilling hosts out of their minds.[29]

This random violence was identical to that described of mid 1930s Mexico by Graham Greene in his despairing travelogue, *Lawless Roads*:

One Sunday in Ortzaba, police agents followed a child who had been at [the illegal] Mass. She ran from them and they fired and killed her – one of those sudden inexplicable outbursts of brutality common in Mexico. Mexicans are fond of children, but some emanation from the evil Aztec soil seems suddenly to seize the brain like drunkenness, then the pistol comes out.[30]

When he wrote his book, Greene was in a state of loathing towards Mexico, and outraged enough by the misery and degradation he had seen there to talk in terms of 'emanations' as the cause of casual, pointless violence. His explanation is not much more far-fetched than some of those found in the psychological literature. According to one survey of the literature, 'violence is always expressive, of emotions of hate or rage, or instrumental, designed to achieve some specific purpose. Senseless violence is only the product of individual or group hysteria, or extreme psychosis.'[31] Neither Greene's mystical explanation nor the sober-sided reassurances of the psychologists would have given any comfort to the victims of violence: they knew they were being attacked by *soldiers*, and they knew they did not deserve it.

THE EFFECTS OF MILITARY VIOLENCE

Some parts of China were less susceptible than others to soldier violence. Places garrisoned by well-disciplined troops enjoyed some degree of security provided the demands of the military institution were met. Places garrisoned by local troops got off fairly lightly, because local men were less likely to prey on their own people. Some areas were so remote that they enjoyed the 'pleasure of having no soldiers' (*wubing zhi fu*). Most areas were not so lucky; they lived continuously with the grey rats and grey wolves. Even worse, they saw continual changes in the actual garrison force. Dali (Shaanxi) was garrisoned by twenty-five units in succession between 1912 and 1930.[32] Towns like this could never be secure. The timing and the nature of soldier violence was unpredictable, but it was never far away.

Soldiers were most dangerous to civilians when they were occupying or evacuating a place; they were more dangerous as groups than as individuals, because the group gave its members the courage to behave badly. The real horror was the unpredictability; it produced a constant state of tension and insecurity, which had damaging effects above and beyond the actual violence.

To some extent the wealthy could protect themselves, by building walls, hiring guards, installing iron bars and bolts (the New York City syndrome). This kind of protection was inadequate against really determined looters, and was no final insurance against the fear of violence. The wealthy could also transfer themselves and their property to foreign protection; they could move to treaty ports, or find local foreigners willing to lend them sanctuary under a foreign flag. Missionaries routinely did this, for free; other foreigners were less scrupulous. In Guangzhou (1924) there were foreigners who assumed nominal ownership of Chinese property to make it immune from Chinese attack.[33] The French consul at Longzhou (Guangxi) rented space in his compound to distressed Chinese civilians whenever an emergency arose.[34]

The poor had no access to such protection (unless they were Christians). They were the most frequent victims of soldiers, the victims of direct attack, looting, theft and rape. It was the poor who were dragged off as coolies for the army, an especially terrifying fate because there was no guarantee that they would return (see appendix 6). Sha Ting's account of the desolation of a mother and her children after her husband's press-ganging for coolie work is a fictional account of something that happened often, sudden, shattering loss almost as bad as an actual death. It was also the poor who bore the brunt of requisitioning, as we saw above.[35]

The poor were generally helpless before the onslaught of soldiers (see appendix 7). Occasionally they tried to resist, or to avenge themselves. In 1920 the people of Hengxian (Guangxi) fell savagely on Cantonese stragglers making their way back to Guangdong after the defeat of their army, and murdered as many as they could. But such acts of revenge depended on finding soldiers alone or in small groups.[36] Organised resistance was much more difficult. Who was to lead it? Local gentry and their militia units were useless, for they preferred to appease soldiers; if they did fall out, it was usually over a demarcation dispute, not because the militia had come to the defence of the local population.[37] Popular, semi-secret organisations such as the Red Spears sometimes organised resistance; in 1929 there were reports of members of the society in action against soldiers in Shaanxi and Shanxi.[38] In 1935, in Huolu (Hebei), the White Spears (*Baiqiang hui*) turned the table on a Shanxi requisitioning attempt by kidnapping the officer sent to demand contributions from the county, carving off bits of his body and sending them one by one to the army headquarters until, after three days, the Shanxi troops decided to move elsewhere.[39] Even commanders who had close connections with the secret society world sometimes found themselves confronted with opposition led by popular organisations. Between 1919 and 1920 peasants in Sangzhi (Hunan) formed their own 'spirit army' (*shenjun*), to resist the demands of the local military for labour conscripts. They refused to be pacified or bought off; they were eventually put down by He Long who had just finished his transformation from bandit to soldier.[40]

Less drastic forms of resistance also occurred – flight, concealment, evasion. Peasants in Qixian (Henan) maimed their draft animals in 1930 so that soldiers would no longer want to confiscate them.[41] People hid or fled when troops were moving through their areas, but this was no defence against garrison troops. The most common response to soldiers was a sullen docility, a recognition that there was little to be done about the grey rats and grey wolves.

7

BAD IRON

He who makes war his profession cannot be
otherwise than vicious. War makes thieves and
peace brings them to the gallows.

                                    Niccolò Machiavelli

It is better to have no son than one
who is a soldier.

                                    Chinese proverb

My men are the scum of the earth.

                                    Duke of Wellington

These statements, from different countries and different periods,
have one thing in common: they assume that soldiers are bad men,
tough, essentially criminal, unworthy members of a decent family or
society. The assumption is that soldiers have characteristics of mind
and behaviour which set them apart from ordinary men, that there is
a special soldier mentality which is base, violent and at odds with
civilian society.

In traditional China, and in the warlord period, soldiers were
assigned a whole series of negative characteristics, which can be
lumped together as 'bad iron' (from the proverb 'Good iron does not
make nails, good men do not make soldiers'). They can also be
looked at separately, for the range of negative characteristics was
very wide, and they were applied to different types of individual
soldier.

A common assumption was that soldiers were stupid dolts, rustic
hayseeds without a glimmer of knowledge or cultivation. Feng
Yuxiang's soldiers, usually taken to be the top of the line amongst
warlord troops, were described (in 1922) as 'morons', 'teenage
automotans' so ignorant that they thought electric fans worked by

magic.[1] Elly Widler, a Swiss adventurer imprisoned by Sichuanese soldiers in 1924, also stressed the idea of abysmal ignorance:

The soldiers all believed that the bullets from their imported foreign guns and from the rifles manufactured in the Chengtu arsenal have eyes and that the bullets hit only those who deserve to die.[2]

This ignorance was not simply mocked; it was perceived as dangerous, because it made soldiers malleable, poor and blank creatures who could be pushed in any direction their commanders chose. They were so stupid that they lacked even a sense of self-preservation.

It is because of their lack of intelligence that these troops proved such good fighting men, the incompetence of their officers and the lack of coordination in the fighting not being fully apparent to them.[3]

'These troops' were Wu Peifu's men, fighting at Shanhaiguan in 1924. Being too stupid to see their own interests carried the implication that they were also too stupid to understand the interests of others, the nation or the civilian population.

Stupidity could be doltishness, mental deficiency, or it could be a brutal, moronic sadism. Wilder described one of his captors who fitted this picture of cretinous brutality:

He was a most extraordinary young man, this Yang Mow; he was only a young fellow, about twenty-two; he had a round face and was always laughing. He could tell you the most horrible tales of atrocity and murder in which he had taken part, and he would giggle all the time.[4]

Soldiers like Yang Mow killed, wounded and pillaged to satisfy some deep but incoherent need in their tiny, evil minds.

Mentally deficient evil was one step away from deliberate sadism, where stupidity was outweighed by conscious malevolence. Here the soldier was seen as the man too wicked to live in civilised society, so depraved that he was evicted from the decent world into the army.[5] This view told civilians why they suffered from soldiers, and at the same time it told them that they were morally superior to them. It was close to the views of soldiers widely held in Victorian England, when armies were still composed of mercenaries:

Every reckless, wild, debauched young fellow, the refuse of the beershop, the sweepings of the gaol, everyone who is too idle to work, too stupid to hold his place among his fellows, who had come into unwelcome contact with the law, or generally involved his fortunes in some desperate calamity, is considered, by general consent, to have a distinct vocation to defend his country.[6]

In other words, going into the army was a public admission of bad character, an announcement that a young man was unfit for civilian society. Enlistment meant voluntarily branding the word 'scum' on one's forehead.

These views of a soldier's mental characteristics and capabilities encouraged the idea that soldiers were born, not made – the 'bad boy' theory of soldier formation. Only violent, anti-social types went into the army (along with the morons). This description could easily be applied to many well-known soldiers, from Zhang Zongchang, who had been a reckless, wild adolescent, to Cao Gun, whose youthful behaviour, especially his gambling, was so outrageous that his family threw him out and into the army.[7]

Zhou Wen gives a fictional account of a 'bad boy' in his short story 'Younger brother' ('Didi'). The main character is a wild, uncontrollable street kid, the second son of a virtuous widow who devotes all her energies to the education of her first son, a 'good boy' of modest talent and impeccable behaviour. Didi is neglected, and to punish his mother he becomes the terror of the village; by the time he is thirteen his behaviour is so impossible that he is sent into the army, his natural home.[8] (See appendix 2.)

The stereotype of bad character led inexorably to expectations of bad behaviour. Once a bad character was in the army, it went without question that his evil traits would be manifested in evil behaviour. Men in uniforms, with guns, were expected to be brutal, and they were feared and detested as such whether they were or not. Zhang Guotas's description of his family's attitude towards soldiers deals with late Qing soldiers; it was an attitude which grew stronger, not weaker, as soldiers multiplied in the warlord period:

My family elders, along with everyone else in the village, had always despised troops. To them troops were a perverse crew of monstrous barbarians, too weak to suppress bandits, but quite strong enough to bully the people: and the mere presence of the Green Standards left them stupefied with fear. Receiving the braves in hastily donned court robes, our elders tried to pacify them by being humble. Nobody dared to protest the soldiers' belligerence. It was a perfect example of the Chinese saying that 'when a soldier and scholar meet, reason is on the soldier's side'.[9]

The cringing timorousness of a powerful gentry family like the Zhangs underscored how profound and pervasive were fear, hatred and contempt of soldiers in China, and how powerful was the in-built assumption that soldiers would terrorise civilians. The only conceivable means of dealing with soldiers was to placate them, to treat them with what amounted to respect, though a respect based on fear, not admiration.

Officers often shared civilian views of soldier depravity. The lists of prohibitions which the Guomindang issued periodically to its soldiers were founded on assumptions about normal soldier behaviour. At various times, Feng Yuxiang issued prohibitions to his troops. They ranged from the very general: 'It is forbidden to drink, smoke, consort with prostitutes, gamble or commit any other illegal act'; 'It is impermissible to beat or curse civilians' – to the specific: 'When conducting transactions with merchants, soldiers may not go behind the counter'; 'Soldiers must buy tickets when travelling by train.'[10] In 1926 Guomindang soldiers were commanded not to seize coolies, not to loot, not to steal provisions, not to commandeer houses.[11] Twenty years later, the list was longer; of the twelve prohibitions, four referred to soldier treatment of civilians. There was to be no cheating the common people, no forcible entry into private homes, no arrogance or churlishness, and no rape or murder.[12]

The behaviour of soldiers which civilians dreaded and the Guomindang hoped to prevent was not a matter of theory. Many soldiers were quite as bad as they were believed and expected to be. Soldiers were far more likely to be callous, sadistic and greedy than they were to be upright and decent. That is why the well-disciplined people's soldiers of the Red Army and the P.L.A. came as such a welcome change. For most people there was little interest in working out why soldiers were as ghastly as they were; it was enough to have to suffer from them. There were sources, however, and several different possible explanations, of the soldier mentality.

The most banal, and the most ironic, is that soldiers simply behaved according to the popular stereotypes of themselves, that they lived up to people's expectations of them. The fundamental aversion to soldiers within Chinese culture had the paradoxical effect of producing men who preyed on their society. This was a vicious circle, for the worse soldiers behaved, the more they were hated and feared, and the more they justified those feelings. So long as the circle was regarded as immutable, it was hard to break it.

Another rather vacuous interpretation saw the reason for the bad behaviour of soldiers as age – soldiers were equated with rebellious teenagers. Here is a report from Guide in 1923 entitled 'Henan's boy rogues': 'So many of the soldiers in this part of the country are young lads in their teens that one wonders if all their self-assertiveness and insolence are not merely a manifestation of the gang spirit.'[13] This would be a nice explanation if it were not so inappropriate to Chinese rural society, where the luxury of a period of teenage rebellion was denied to all but the sons of the affluent, the least likely candidates for service in the army ranks. It would also imply that all Chinese soldiers were very young, which they were not. Army careers could be very long.

The only explanation which covers the majority of soldiers is one which concentrates on their experience in the army rather than looking at the attributes they brought with them on recruitment. This assumes that soldiers learnt their brutal ways in the army, that the army itself was the breeding-ground of the soldier mentality.

Zhu Zhixin, the early Guomindang leader, was the author of this explanation of the soldier mentality, though he did not talk of 'mentality' but of 'abnormal psychology' (*biantai xinli*). Zhu's very active military and political career did not prevent him from continually widening his intellectual range. His sensitive and supple mind had been opened to an awareness of underlying psychological patterns, and the ways in which these patterns could be perverted and distorted. His openness of mind was matched by a deep compassion for men he had actually commanded, who in their own way were victims of the peculiar historical conditions of early Republican China.

According to Zhu, soldiers were not by nature cruel and violent. They learnt their behaviour in the army. 'Good men suddenly became bad men.'[14] They became violent when they entered a nascent military society in which soldiers themselves were treated violently by their officers, and in which there were few sanctions or prohibitions against violent behaviour towards civilians.

In his article 'The abnormal psychology of the soldier', Zhu described how young men were systematically brutalised in the army, turned from 'normal' into 'abnormal' human beings.[15] The combination of their maltreatment, especially as recruits, and the danger of their lives as fighters, stripped away their normal sensitivities and restraints. Their brutal experience at the hands of their superiors, the beatings and cursings which came their way, made them brutal towards those less powerful than themselves.

At the same time as they were being brutalised, they were also being made irresponsible and unthinking. All the decisions about life and livelihood that civilians took routinely were made for them by their officers. The Good Soldier Schweik was an Austrian soldier, but his observations about a soldier's need to think for himself would have fitted his Chinese contemporaries:

Humbly report I don't think because that's forbidden to soldiers on duty. When I was in the 91st Regiment some years ago our captain always used to say: A soldier mustn't think; his superiors do it for him. As soon as a soldier begins to think he's no longer a soldier but a dirty lousy civilian.[16]

Soldiers had no responsibility for themselves, or for anyone else; they were forced to be irresponsible, not to ask questions, think about the future, or question their commander's wisdom or capacity. Theirs was not to reason why, but to follow orders.

This irresponsibility, coupled with their experience of harshness and insecurity in their daily life, made them into casually destructive, wanton creatures, cut off from the norms of civilian behaviour. They broke no codes when they oppressed civilians because there were no codes for them to break. Their psychology had been perverted to the only one the army allowed, which did not encompass a moral code of behaviour.

The Chinese military world of the warlord period was too new and too fragmented to have established formal standards (or informal norms) of behaviour. Soldiers learnt how to behave in an *ad hoc* fashion. They became predatory towards the civilian world not as a matter of policy, but in imitation of the way their commanders treated them and the civilian world. They developed a 'murderous and turbulent psychology' (*shayi yu luanduo xinli*)[17] because that seemed to be the informal norm of the army.

The experience of Shen Congwen as a young recruit shows the process at work. Shen joined the army in his native west Hunan, in a garrison town on the edge of Han territory. Up in the hills further west lived minority peoples, restless, dispossessed and bitter people,

Bad iron

the victims of Han encroachment – but no real threat to Han power. Soon after his enlistment, Shen's unit was sent off on a 'pacification mission'. What the boy of thirteen saw on that campaign still horrified him decades later when he wrote his autobiography. At least 2,000 minority people were butchered, their villages fired, their crops destroyed. The soldiers went on a rampage of murder and arson. 'The only thing our unit had to do was kill. Our soldiers seemed incapable of anything but killing.'[18]

The episode described by Shen was extreme; it involved the ultimate forms of violence, killing and destruction. The victims were minorities, not Han; they always got shorter shrift. But this prejudice was implicit, not explicit. Soldiers were not taught that they could do things to minorities which were taboo for Han. On the contrary, most soldiers never came across minorities. Their victims came precisely from their own pre-army world.

There was in their brutality towards their own kind, in their spasms of violence which often looked pointless, a hidden agenda, a lust for revenge against a world in which they had been impotent as civilians, before they went into the army. Zhu Zhixin saw in their brutality a reaction against the civilian world, an acting out of hostility against a society in which they had been the dregs.[19] Any sense of common origin, of class ties between soldiers and civilians, was destroyed by the power they had as armed men over unarmed ones. By going into the army they had severed their class ties, to become the agents of the military elite dominating China, and at the same time oppressors in their own right, enjoying the pleasures and privileges which the means of violence, provided by their new superiors, gave them. (See appendix 8.)

Zhu did not despair of Chinese soldiers. He believed that decent soldiers could exist, but not in the military structure of his period. The whole pattern of army training and command would have to change before soldiers could be anything but abnormal in their psychology, before the soldier mentality which caused so much grief could be changed. Zhu died (in 1920) before he could have his plans for an improvement in the quality of soldiers implemented. Even if he had lived, he would have had a hard task ahead of him, for he had to confound both the expectations of his fellow-officers, in and out of the Guomindang camp, and of the public at large. So long as everyone expected soldiers to be licensed thugs, that was what they would be.

It suited the army to have terrifying soldiers, because so long as they were feared, the civilian population was quiescent. Civilians could not see beyond their fears; a new type of soldier, and a new attitude towards him, were out of the question.

Some attempts were made to produce a better class of soldier. Feng Yuxiang, Li Zongren, Zhang Fakui and Cai Tingkai were famous for the quality of their troops, and for the humane way they treated them. In the early 1930s the Guomindang, under the instigation of its German advisors, who were very critical of the average calibre of soldiers, made some attempts to produce at least a few units of well-trained, well-behaved men.[20] Most commanders did not. The effort was too great, the rewards in the warlord system too slim. The recognition of need was not there.

The effort required to produce well-behaved soldiers whom civilians could respect would have been huge. Even in well-run armies with strict codes of behaviour, there are fundamental distortions. A society made up of males only is bound to be abnormal. The lack of normal personal relationships with parents, wives and children may lead to the formation of abnormal ones. Homosexuality is a standard feature of many armies – though not, according to any evidence I have seen, of Chinese ones; this may have been one taboo which could not be broken, or a secret too shocking to record on paper. The all-male world can also produce relations of comradeship and mutual care which amount to fictive familial relationships. Intense, long-lasting friendships may come out of lives of shared danger. For the right type of man, soldiering is the best life, a communal, disciplined life with a mixture of hard work and hard play, respectful deference and kindly command.[21] (This definition of soldiering came from 'Mad Mike' Hoare, a present-day mercenary currently in jail in South Africa.) But it is achieved at the cost of the atrophy of other emotions, and of a lack of concern for people beyond the army world.

The joys of soldiering were not the norm in Chinese armies. There was no tradition of all-boys-together, no regimental pride, no *esprit de corps*. These could not grow in a system where men were disposable, officers and men sharply divided, and discipline based on punishment, not natural respect. Only the social and emotional isolation from civilian life was real, and it was compounded by the enforced idleness of barrack life, with limited training and guard duty, and only occasional episodes of action. The release from boredom was to use one's guns to victimise civilians, and thus to reinforce the stereotype of 'bad iron'.

8

LEAVING THE ARMY

Old soldiers never die, they only fade away.

A society which maintains a large military establishment, and keeps its soldiers in service for a fixed period of time, can expect to have a large number of veterans. In communist China such men have acted as important props to the state, serving in administrative and para-military positions throughout Chinese society. Just the fact that they often continue to wear their uniforms (without insignia) gives them an air of authority and toughness. In warlord China the term 'veteran' was virtually meaningless. There were only ex-soldiers (*tuiwu bing*), men who had left the ranks. Men left in so many ways that the idea of routine honourable discharges at the end of a fixed period of service had no currency. They were disbanded, they were defeated and found themselves without an army to serve in, they were dismissed by their officers or they deserted. Wage soldiers stayed in the army as long as it suited them, or as long as there was an army for them to serve in.

Desertion was a standard way out of the army. It was not an approved method of departure, and deserters could be punished very severely, but most commanders made little strenuous effort to stop it. They accepted it as a form of natural selection, which removed from the army men who would rather not be there, and who presumably, because of their discontent, did not make very useful soldiers. Desert-ers were seldom pursued; if they got out of the area their commander controlled they were home free anyhow, for there was no nationwide system of military police to look for deserters. It was hard sometimes to tell when a soldier's extended leave, to help his family with the farm work at busy times, had turned into desertion. Such lengthy leaves were regularly given to married soldiers; their wives could manage for most of the year, but needed them back for planting and harvest. Commanders were willing to accommodate these needs, provided the military situation was quiet at the time.[1] Sometimes the soldier came back, sometimes not.

Some deserters were caught and punished. Sha Ting's chilling story of the execution of a captured deserter by his own brother (see appendix 6), who was serving in the same unit, is not completely fictional, though it is exceptionally macabre.[2] But desertion was so common that it made more sense to concentrate on new recruitment rather than on bothering with bad blood. In addition to expanding the number of soldiers, recruitment replaced those who had deserted: 'It has been said on good Chinese authority that if recruiting were dropped for five years, there would be nothing left of the Chinese army but the officers.'[3] This comment by a foreign observer in 1924 was echoed by Li Zongren in 1928; he estimated that desertion normally took fifty per cent of the strength of a unit within a single year.[4] (He did not indicate whether this included his own command or not, but he did not specifically exclude it.)

The Military Commission of the Guomindang regularly published long lists of the names and descriptions of deserters in the Military Gazette: the descriptions did not provide the kind of detail which would suggest that deserters were actively pursued. They were usually limited to name, age, unit, rank and county of origin. Only occasionally were physical descriptions included, and then their usefulness was limited by the physical homogeneity of the soldier population. There were no real distinctions in height, and only impressionistic ones in physiognomy; faces could be long, thin, square or round in shape, black, yellow or white in complexion.[5] Very occasionally the name of a guarantor (*baoren*) was published, along with his address (a street address, which was never listed for the actual deserters), presumably so that financial redress could be sought from the guarantor. Most of the deserters appear not to have had guarantors.[6]

Why did men desert so often? The obvious reason was that it was so easy to do so. A man did not have to think all that carefully about enlistment if he knew he could come out of the army very easily. He could enlist, see whether the army suited him or not, and then stay or desert. The ease of desertion allowed many enlistments to be informal probationary exercises. The average length of service for men who deserted from the Nanjing Garrison (1928) was six months; that included a number of men who stayed only two weeks.[7]

The ease of desertion made it possible for men to desert, but they did so for specific reasons. In 1895 the Newly Established Army published a list of reasons why men were unhappy in the army and deserted; it was a list which applied very well to later periods as well:

1. Inability to get leave to deal with family problems
2. Poor relations with fellow-soldiers
3. Poor relations with officers
4. Problems which could not be discussed with others
5. Indebtedness
6. Stealing
7. Breach of army regulations
8. Inability to put up with hardship
9. Poor prospects of a soldier's unit
10. Poor individual prospects
11. Regret at having enlisted in a fit of pique.[8]

These reasons are comprehensive and self-explanatory (except for the mysterious no. 4); the soldiers found life in the army too hard, or were in trouble, either in the army or at home. These deserters were men who had run afoul of the army system, or who should not have enlisted in the first place. Men who had gone in involuntarily usually left at the first opportunity. Almost all the young men who were press-ganged in Chengdu in 1926 were gone within a month.[9] This was the reason why armies tended to press-gang only in acute emergencies; they knew they could not keep men recruited in this way.

The desertions discussed above took place in normal times, when the army was not actually fighting. The prospect of battle gave mercenaries additional cause to ask themselves whether they should stay in the army or not. All soldiers need powerful incentives to get them into battle, and keep them in line while it lasts. The most powerful are religious or political commitment, a sense of *noblesse oblige* or hero worship of the commander. Less lofty but just as powerful incentives are fear of officers, and the punishment they can impose; fear of the enemy, and what he will do if not defeated; and lust for loot, the rewards of the battlefield; 'Dutch courage' can also work wonders by blurring the edges of reality.[10] Very few of these incentives worked well on mercenaries serving in poorly organised armies, fighting against enemies who were also mercenaries.

Astute mercenaries calculated the likelihood of their unit's success in battle; if the odds were poor, it made sense to go early, before things got dangerous. Cai Tingkai and his comrades deserted from their unit just before it went into battle (in 1917); by going early, they had no difficulty in getting away with their rifles, which they sold for 80 *yuan* each. The feebler-minded who stayed on to fight were defeated, disbanded and got only 3 *yuan* each to get them home.[11] At the officer level, this kind of realistic assessment of the probable outcome of a battle was called taking the silver bullet – i.e. arranging for a cash payment from the opposing side not to fight, or to change sides during the course of battle. The men made their decision by deserting.

Deserting during battle was more complicated. It was determined in part by the configuration of the battle. Men on the flanks or in the rear had better chances to desert than men in the front line, when getting out of battle meant running the gauntlet of one's own guns as well as the enemy's. Desertion in battle was common enough, however, for warlord officers to lead from the rear, as the simplest means of preventing desertion – and of protecting themselves.[12]

The most likely scenario for desertion in battle was the breakaway of a large body of troops when they began to feel that their side was losing. This was less a question of deserting from battle than of avoiding further risk of death or injury. The inducement of a sense of impending defeat was a major tactical skill in the arsenal of a commander. In 1927 Bai Baoshan took the field in Zhejiang against the advancing Guomindang armies, his soldiers marching under his personal banners with the single character 'Bai' on them. Soon after the battle started his men saw the same banners on the enemy side; they assumed that part of Bai Baoshan's army had gone over to the other side, and immediately departed from the battlefield. In fact the banners belonged to Bai Chongxi, the Guomindang commander.[13]

Mercenary soldiers who deserted in battle were behaving as sensible employees; they preferred not to risk their skins for their employer, especially if he seemed about to lose. Unless he could keep them on the field with the promise of loot or other future reward, it made sense to go. Principled soldiers (*zhuyi bing*) of the Guomindang Northern Expeditionary forces terrified warlord commanders who encountered them just because they were unlikely to desert in battle.

The fate of deserters was seldom traumatic. No stigma of a moral kind attached to deserting. They could either go home, find another unit to enlist in (in which case they would usually wait around near the battlefield) or go into banditry. Their decision depended on whether they had had enough of the army, or just of one particular unit. They did not leave empty-handed; they always had their uniform, often a weapon and sometimes bedding.[14] These goods could either be sold for cash, or used as entry cards into another armed force, legal or illegal.

Defeated soldiers were in a more difficult situation. The fact that they had not deserted was an indication that they felt they had nowhere else to go. Unless they could quickly find another commander to take them on, they were stranded. Sometimes they were in acute danger, not from other soldiers but from local civilians who saw their chance to revenge themselves on weakened men. This was especially the case when the course of battle had split men into small groups. When Xiong Kewu lost Chengdu in 1924, his troops found themselves the targets of the civilians they had been oppressing before. In a rush to get rid of their soldier identity, they stripped off their uniforms, threw their guns into public conveniences and tried to look like ordinary, if partially dressed, civilians.[15]

Deserters who had only been in the army for a brief period might well go home and be reassimilated into civilian life, but long-serving deserters or defeated soldiers were most likely to look for a new unit or to go into the bandit world. A man who had been in the military world for a long time was hard to reabsorb into the non-military world. He was used to military life, was at home there and found it hard to make decisions for himself. He was no longer used to hard physical labour or to material insecurity, both of which waited for him outside the army. He would try to stay in the military world, either as a lawful soldier or as an outlaw. The only way to get committed soldiers out of the army permanently, before old age or death took them out, was to disband them.

Disbandment meant a formal process of declaring a certain proportion of soldiers surplus to need, severing them from the army, and returning them to civilian life with adequate compensation for their service to enable them to make a new start in life. From 1912 onwards, there was never much doubt that China had more soldiers than she needed or could afford. There were constant calls for large-scale disbandment, and detailed schemes for what to do with disbanded soldiers. The schemes were usually designed to solve at least two problems at once. One proposed organising ex-soldiers into engineering gangs, to build roads, dykes and bridges, modernising the country while reducing military expenditures.[16] No-one liked this idea very much, least of all the intended participants. Feng Yuxiang and Yan Xishan both favoured the widely promoted idea of using ex-soldiers to open up virgin land in the North-West; military colonies would be set up to work the land and to provide a defensive presence against foreign incursion.[17] Another proposal was to disband some soldiers and hire them as coolies to carry goods for the army, giving employment to ex-soldiers and making conscription of coolies unnecessary.[18]

None of these schemes had much chance of success. The disbandment proposals of politicians, in or out of government, were accurately described as 'trendy fanfares' (*liuxing de gaodiao*).[19] The people who wanted disbandment, government officials and politicians worried about military expenditures, intellectuals concerned about the fate of the nation, and ordinary people burdened by their sufferings at the hands of soldiers, were powerless to bring it about. The men who had the capacity to do it, the army commanders, and the men who would be disbanded, the soldiers, were unenthusiastic.

There was some disbandment after the 1911 Revolution, when irregular soldiers were unceremoniously pushed out of the Republican forces, but very little thereafter. The Disbandment Sub-Committee of the Washington Conference held sessions in Beijing in 1922, with no noticeable effect.[20] The Disbandment Conference held in 1928 after the end of the Northern Expedition amounted to four days of sitting and chatting (*zuotan*).[21] The formal disbandment activities produced a lot of 'bumf', rancorous disagreements and at most the dismissal of a few old and decrepit soldiers.

The objections of commanders to disbandment were self-interested; their soldiers were their chief resource, and their quantity mattered more than their quality. A general with 50,000 mediocre troops felt much stronger than one with 5,000 crack troops. Disbandment meant emasculation; they were willing to advocate it for others, but not to try it themselves.[22] A commander also had to consider what would happen to soldiers he let go. If they enlisted with his rivals he would be stabbing himself in the back. If they became bandits, he might have to 'pacify' them.

The Nanjing government wanted to disband troops not under direct central control.[23] Other authorities disagreed; to surrender their troops meant surrendering to the central government. Petty independent commanders were unwilling to give up a single man. Subordinate officers were frightened of disbandment; if the men under their command were disbanded, they became surplus themselves. There were so many unemployed officers about, men whose units had been defeated, products of military schools without jobs, that being surplus meant being on the scrap-heap, cut off from the considerable privileges of being an officer. Only substantial compensation could reconcile them to the loss of their jobs. That was too expensive. Other schemes for retraining officers for new jobs, recycling them into new lines or simply retiring them, required such large outlays that it was cheaper to keep them in the army.[24] Keeping them on implied keeping the men they commanded.

Soldiers were usually as opposed to disbandment as their officers. The ease of desertion meant that those who did not want to stay could go; the corollary was that those who stayed did so from choice, and did not want to leave. A man who had been in the army for many years would probably be out of touch with his family and friends, people who might ease the return to civilian life. Disbandment meant being thrown out of his surrogate family, the army, alone and with little likelihood of making a living. A man who had enlisted because he was unemployed or unhappily employed in the civilian world was no more likely to find satisfactory work after disbandment. Unless they had learnt a trade (as mechanics, drivers, telegraph operators, cooks etc.) ex-soldiers were less likely to find adequate employment than they had been before enlistment. Army life sapped the work ethic. It was generally held that ex-soldiers were almost unemployable:

Excepting in some few regiments, he has received no training and undergone no drill. His days have been spent in loafing about the streets, which has inculcated, if not increased, a distaste for regular work. (1914)

Although these [Fujian] troops were raised from the civilian world, they have been acculturated to the military world and have completely lost the capacity to make a living. (1926)[25]

The uncertainties of the civilian world contrasted poorly with the security of the army, the lack of day-to-day anxiety over food and shelter. The loss of power which accompanied leaving the army was not something to be relished. Appeals to soldiers to be patriotic, to save China from the scourge of soldiers by abandoning their parasitic lives and letting themselves be disbanded fell on deaf ears.[26]

The antipathy to disbandment is pointed up by the numerous occasions on which soldiers violently resisted disbandment or went straight from disbandment into another unit. In Zhenzhou (Hunan) in 1914, soldiers mustered for disbandment mutinied and shot their commander.[27] (Whether they stayed in the army or not after that was not reported.) In 1923 Henan troops who had been involuntarily disbanded kidnapped five missionaries and ordered them 'to use their influence with the government to get them reinstated in the regular army'. The missionaries agreed to do so, on condition that their captors listened to the preaching of the gospel.[28] Thirty thousand Zhejiang troops, disbanded after defeat in 1924, went straight into other armies.[29] To these men, the army was an iron rice bowl.

The final irony of disbandment was that though in theory it was the only answer to China's problem of excessive soldiers, in practice it was as unpopular with civilians as it was with officers and men. Civilians and civil authorities feared the disruption and violence of ex-soldiers. They pleaded with commanders not to disband men on their patch. If that failed, they were willing to pay to have them sent somewhere else. Six regiments of Anhui, Henan and Jiangsu troops disbanded in Shanxi in 1916 were loaded on to trains and shipped out of the province at government expense.[30] The provincial government preferred to pay to have them taken away, anywhere but Shanxi, rather than see them on the loose in the province.

Throughout the warlord period, disbandment was discussed, but almost never implemented. The only major forms of departure from the army were desertion and retirement. Retirement was not straightforward. Few armies paid pensions, and except for (rare) retirement bonuses, soldiers who retired were on their own. Only the accumulation of wealth through loot and savings could guarantee a comfortable retirement. But army life was not conducive to making careful plans for the future. Soldiers lived in tight-knit groups, followed orders and made no decisions for themselves. Their life made them dependent, psychologically and materially, and stripped them of the capacity to control their own lives. This fecklessness (*wanshi bu guan*) promised them a hard life outside the army, where fecklessness led to destitution.[31] The violent behaviour which became second nature in the army was unacceptable in the civilian world, where it only worked if backed by a gun and a uniform. The dangers and insecurities of army life were powerful but limited – basically the dangers were officers and the enemy in battle. Soldiers learnt ways of coping with them. In civilian life the enemies were many, and difficult to manipulate, appease or avoid – landlords, officials, the gentry, the weather, the market, insects, bandits, soldiers. It made sense to try to stay in the army as long as possible.

The relative ease of army life meant that men often stayed in for a long while. Middle-aged and elderly soldiers were outnumbered by youthful ones, but were quite common. A man whose forty-sixth anniversary in the army was celebrated in 1947 was unusual – he was named in a Guomindang army journal as 'China's Number One Old Soldier' (*Zhongguo diyi ming laobing*)[32] – but service of twenty years or more was not uncommon. Soldiers who stayed healthy, were not wounded and were capable of performing light duties were found a niche.

One practice which looked at first sight like disbandment, and was often claimed as such, was what might be called a reassignment, from direct to indirect involvement with the army. Those concerned were the middle-aged men who started working for the army rather than in it. This is a description of a garrison town just north of Chengdu (Sichuan):

Aside from the regular soldiers, all the other people in the town were obviously in plain clothes. All the small traders were disbanded aides, staff officers, junior officers or soldiers of the Sichuan army. After they left the army, they had no livelihood, so had to start a small business. Because of their special connections, they managed not to pay taxes, to 'borrow' by force from civilians, to take over civilian houses, so most of them had a useful line they could pursue. It had become standard for disbanded officers and men to go into business.[33]

Old soldiers did not die; they merely faded into the fringes of the army world.

9

MILITARISM
AND CHRONIC VIOLENCE

A major preoccupation of traditional Chinese philosophy and state-craft was the avoidance of disorder, and the outlawing of confusion. Though the state might use force as a final arbiter, the authority of the state was vested not in the sword but in the writing brush of the scholar-official. The state and its servants were capable of great violence, but did not practise it as the preferred means of control. In the eighteenth century, China stood apart and aloof as a haven of civility in contrast to the rest of the turbulent world. In the twentieth century, she found herself plunged into several decades of miserable turbulence, in which soldiers, the trained agents of violence, took over control from civilians. China found herself, if not in a general reign of terror, at least in a prolonged period of chronic violence.

VIOLENCE AS A THEORETICAL PROBLEM

In a world beset by violence, a major interest in the study of violence has developed. Violence in the home (battered wives, battered babies), violence against women, criminal violence, terrorist violence, sports violence, media violence, the violence of warfare – these are some of the sub-species of violence which have received particular attention. The effect of chronic violence, of living in a society where violence is always threatening, has received much less attention, though this state of affairs is the norm in any society in which an undisciplined or divided military is in power. Today this means most of Central America, much of Latin America and Africa, the Lebanon, Iran, the Philippines. In the 1920s and 1930s the chronic misery of lawless soldiery afflicted Mexico, much of the Balkans – and China.

Few of the theories on violence help to explain situations of chronic violence, especially ones in which the ostensible guardians of order have become the chief agents of violence. The violence usually seems so complicated, so arcane and yet so pointless that it defies analysis, and arouses only reactions of disgust. Scholars are often drawn into more controllable fields of study.

One field looks at man's animal nature, at his instinctual behaviour, in search of evidence that *homo sapiens* is naturally violent. (I say 'his', because in the animal world, only the female hampster is more aggressive than the male; in all other species, aggresion, the propensity for violence, is equated with maleness.[1]) In animals, and in animalian human behaviour, violence can be seen to have some practical attributes, in terms of the survival of the fittest, and of the sharing of scarce resources through spatial distribution of a species.

These ethological approaches are fascinating, but of limited use in understanding the behaviour of highly socialised human beings. Man's basic aggression may have primitive origins, but social evolution has transformed the ways in which violence is manifested.

Most obviously, the use of weapons has transformed man's capacity to inflict violence. The capacity of man-as-animal to deliver violence is very limited, as a British psychologist appropriately named Gunn describes vividly:

It is extremely difficult for one naked unarmed man to kill another such man. He has to resort to strangulation, or to punching him hard enough to knock him over so that he may gash open an important vessel with his teeth, or break his head open by dashing it against the ground... Weapons magnify the aggressivity of a creature many times.[2]

It is possible to match individual categories of weapons with man's unconscious nature, as the Italian psychoanalyst Franco Fornari has done. He equates swords and spears with genital-sadistic fantasies, firearms with anal sadism, and nuclear weapons with oral sadism.[3] These associations mystify rather than clarify the use and effects of violence.

To explain why violence occurs, and why situations of chronic violence emerge, we need to look at social and economic factors. There are a number of readily available explanations along these lines. One is that violence is essentially class based, that it is the means by which elements of a class society are kept in place – those at the top use violence or the threat of it to keep their subordinates in thrall. This view would explain the violence of state authorities, in which the agents of violence – army and police – become the pawns of political masters in maintaining the social and economic status quo. Another theory sees violence as a spasmodic affair, rather like an infection. The reign of violence of the Nazi period, or the fury of the Cultural Revolution, may be explained in these terms, as aberrations from a peaceable normality. Both these theories are self-serving: they explain away violence, rather than explaining why it occurs.

One popular theory which seems tailor-made for China sees violence as a by-product of overcrowding. This theory, based on observations of rats living in extreme overcrowding, sees violence as a reaction to acute stress. It can be extended to explain the violence of warfare as a means of eliminating surplus population and restoring a proper balance between man and his resources. Given that the period of chronic violence we are concerned with came on the heels of the explosive population growth in China in the eighteenth and nineteenth centuries, it seems a tempting explanation. But it is contradicted by the fact that violence was least severe in the most crowded parts of China, the burgeoning cities, and worst in some of the least crowded areas, such as the hills of North China. Violence was never spread evenly across the country.

This unevenness of distribution might indicate another approach to the explanation of violence, an ecological one. This suggests that there are permanent pools of violence, where social and economic conditions have come together to make violence endemic. This argument has been persuasively presented by Elizabeth Perry in her study of the Huai-Bei region.[4] These pools certainly existed, miserable, festering areas in which the problem of violence was intractable. But in warlord China, violence and the threat of it spread their pall far beyond the few traditional pools. It appeared, moreover, in only a few guises, and not in the wide range of forms which characterised the pools of violence. Its major form was the violence of armed men, principally soldiers, against civilians. The growth of violence was the result of militarism, a direct concomitant of the institutional vacuum which was a key feature of warlord domination.

VIOLENCE IN WARLORD CHINA

The forms of violence which blossomed in warlord China were

limited. There has been some speculation that domestic violence, specifically against women, increased dramatically in the Republic, but there is no evidence to back it up.[5] There seems to have been some increase in crime, or at least in the reporting of it, but not in violent crime. Statistics for Peking show a 46.7 increase in crime over a four year period (1913–17), from 2,549 to 3,886 incidents, but since this was a time of rapid population growth in the city, the rate per thousand people went up only by just over 1%, from 3.5 to 4.8 per thousand.[6] A later study, conducted in 1928 and 1930 across the country, claimed that China was in the middle of a crime wave, but showed that increase almost entirely in the area of 'economic' crime: 'Crimes of misappropriation and theft increased tremendously, while crimes of violence and sexual immorality remained nearly constant.'[7] This author confidently connected crime with the malevolent impact of the West on China. He saw crime as 'a very significant, if not the most significant manifestation of the disorganisation in China following upon contact with the West'.[8] This view of western contagion has always had a vogue in China; its current manifestation is in the attack on moral pollution (*jingshen wuran*). It cannot be dismissed as ethnocentric prejudice. One form of clear borrowing is soccer hooliganism, which erupted in China in 1981 after the China–Yemen football match in which China won an unexpected victory. That was late in the day. Long before that, from the middle of the nineteenth century, western impact had combined with internal decay to bring down the ancient civil institutions of the Chinese Empire.

It was this collapse of civil institutions, underway before the fall of the Qing in 1911, and accelerated thereafter, which paved the way for the growth of chronic violence. Into the institutional void left by the collapse of the old systems came militarism, and a form of society which Samuel Huntington calls praetorian society, in which the military rules, and its violence is subject to no checks because none exist.[9] The power of the military fills the void, but not in a stop-gap sense, because once entrenched it is almost impossible to dislodge.

China's descent into warlordism was aggravated by the fact that the West brought to China not only an assault on her institutional fabric, but also the means by which violence could be easily and widely distributed – modern weapons, especially the gun. 'The gun was a great leveller. It can be said to have created the concept of the marginal economic man ... it not only made every soldier an equal threat, it also represented a technique which almost anyone could be taught.'[10] This description, of the introduction of early guns into European armies in the seventeenth century, is applicable to twentieth-century China, or to any society into which easy-to-use weapons are introduced. For the first time, men with limited intelligence, training or skill could become agents of violence, impossible when the dominant weapons were bows, swords or early firearms, all of which required skill and training to use effectively. Modern weapons turned a man into an agent of violence in a brief period and with minimal training. Such men, as soldiers, made possible the existence of predatory military regimes, regimes in which 'military institutions represented a marginally functional role in their societies but claimed an extravagant share of scarce resources'.[11] In China, there were many such regimes, the power bases of individual warlords.

The advent of militarism, and the arming of large numbers of soldiers, made the growth of soldier violence towards civilians possible, but not inevitable. Why were soldiers willing to turn on the civilian population?

The literature on militarism normally treats soldiers as completely lacking in initiative, automata. One authoritative work simply states that it will not deal with sergeants, corporals and enlisted men, because 'these soldiers almost inevitably accept the orders of their officers'.[12] It is officers who shape militarism; the men are their tools.

This may be true of battles, or of military coups, but not of the ways in which militarism is experienced by civilians. Their daily horror is of armed juveniles who respect no normal patterns of behaviour and have apparently betrayed the civilian world into which they were born.

It is generally assumed that the hierarchy of an army parallels civilian hierarchies. To quote Katherine Chorley,

broadly speaking, an army reproduces in its own character the structure of the society in which it grew up. When this is a class structure, this means in practice that the main features of the army character will square with those of the traditionally strongest classes in the community. The corps of officers will be chosen from those classes, and the rank and file will be subjected to a system of discipline and influence to make them so much docile material in the hands of their officers.[13]

There was no such tradition in the Chinese military. What is clear, however, from Jerome Ch'en's *Military/Gentry Coalition*, is that the traditional gentry was increasingly successful about adapting its power holding so that its interests and the interests of the warlords were mutually benefited.[14] What is also clear is that the sense of class consciousness was so feeble amongst the masses that young men who became soldiers had almost no sense of class betrayal. What was remarkable about Chinese soldiers was their massive political indifference, their lack of political involvement in a period of great political flux.

Instead, soldiers were trained to violence, in principle against the military enemies of their commanders, but just as easily against the unarmed civilian world. Their training was augmented, in terms of their likelihood to use violence, by their incorporation into small, closed groups – their units – in which group cohesion encouraged them to accept as normal and even desirable the violence they used against outsiders, soldiers or civilians. They were taught controlled violence, instigated by their officers, with, built in, 'the possibility of uncontrolled violence as release, the drunken and licentious soldiery, hungry for a town to sack'.[15] Army training, plus group behaviour, broke down any inhibitions against the indiscriminate use of violence. As the leading authority on men in groups, Lionel Tiger, puts it: 'Members of groups given power, or having or taking it, may be more able to avoid punishment for aggressive or violent actions than individuals undertaking similar actions should these actions be illegal or immoral in the community'.[16] By Tiger's standard, Chinese soldiers were home free. They had the means of violence, the gun; they had the minimal training necessary for its use; they had the connivance of their officers in using violence against civilians, and the support of their immediate group of fellow-soldiers in doing so. Their only saving grace was their inefficiency. China's real nightmare was to come when she had to deal with soldiers who not only had licence to treat civilians as they liked, but were also efficient at doing so – the soldiers of Imperial Japan. In the mean time, the only solution was to find ways of living with the plague of soldiers.

LIFE WITH CHRONIC MILITARY VIOLENCE

People who live in societies where violence is a constant threat have to develop means of coping with it, or at least minimising it. As you drive into the Canadian Rockies, you are handed a leaflet entitled 'You are entering bear country.' It sets out strict rules of behaviour for those who do not relish an encounter with a grizzly. In New York, the source of danger is human, not animal; newcomers very quickly learn not to go into Central Park after dark, not to use certain subway exits, and never to go to Harlem. They accept iron bars on their windows, and three locks on their front doors. Whether the danger is animal or human, certain basic techniques have to be adopted: avoiding the attention of the source of danger; mapping danger, and keeping out of places which are known to be dangerous; recognising and fleeing from dangerous types of animals or people. These techniques mean the acceptance of major restrictions in order to avoid danger.

Chinese civilians of the warlord period were past masters at managing danger. They avoided the attention of soldiers by hiding from them; incoming soldiers usually found deserted towns or villages. Women, and especially young ones, were kept out of sight. Since conspicuous wealth was an invitation to loot, the rich disguised their wealth behind blank walls. Outside the house, silk jackets were covered with cotton ones, and fur worn only on the inside of winter clothing. Many of these were traditional practices, continued for the sake of security. (Covering silk with cotton continued to be useful under communist rule, when the danger was not theft, but an accusation of being bourgeois.)

The rich could afford to protect their homes with hardware, and to hire armed guards. They could also remove themselves from areas of danger, by moving to foreign concessions, where personal security was much greater. (These concessions were the closest thing to the sanctuary offered in medieval Europe by the church. There was, however, no idea of the Peace of God, which in Europe outlawed violent activity on religious holidays and Sundays.) The poor had far fewer resources to protect themselves against danger, which put them in the front line of soldier violence.

All Chinese had detailed maps of danger, constantly updated through rumour. They knew not to travel alone, to keep away from places where soldiers concentrated, not to travel on trains when soldiers were on the move. The only residents of China who spurned such precautions were missionaries, and they, especially in the early

1920s, were frequently kidnapped for their misplaced faith in the protection of the Lord.

Managing danger protected people, but it also involved them in a continual round of preoccupation which sapped their energy to deal with less obvious threats, or to engage in more productive activities. The effects of the fear of danger and violence were less clear than the direct effects of violence, because they concerned things that did not happen, rather than things which did. The fear of violence against property and of theft deterred the owners of capital from investing in houses, farm buildings, factories or other plant, and encouraged them instead to put their money in safer places, such as land. Productive capital investment was impeded by the fear that the investment might be lost to soldier violence. In developed economies, warfare often has a strongly stimulative effect on the economy because it demands major industrial production in armaments manufacture, shipbuilding, aircraft construction and so on. In China, where the arms industry was tiny, and limited to the production of small arms and ammunition, the growth in this sector was far off-set by the negative effects on other sectors of the industrial economy, created by the climate of insecurity which deterred major investment outside the foreign enclaves.

The fear of violence disrupted internal trade; merchants and their goods were easy prey for armed men. Some commodities could bear the increase in prices which transporting them under guard incurred – notably opium. High-bulk low-price commodities such as grain were hardly worth stealing. Medium-priced, medium-bulk commodities were most vulnerable. One example of trade which almost dried up because of predatory soldiers was the trade in eggs, pigs and poultry between Hunan and Guangdong. After a period in 1923 when these items were routinely seized by soldiers, the trade almost stopped. No seller was willing to make free gifts to the soldiers.[17] Merchants kept away from commercial centres where violence was a threat. In 1920 Li Zongren and his soldiers came into the once-lively market town of Lingshan (Guangdong), to find that the four or five hundred merchants who normally traded there had all departed when the rampaging soldiers of Chen Jiongming arrived, leaving the place a ghost town.[18]

The interruption of trade had its most powerful effect on the weakest links in the trading chain. A journalist who visited the hill town of Songfan, in northern Sichuan, in the summer of 1936 described what had happened there after the town's trading routes had been cut by military activity:

Everywhere in the streets were dead bodies. Outside the town some of the bodies were decomposing, with their innards hanging out, the limbs detached. There were clouds of flies on them, which flew up and buzzed around the heads of passers-by. It was ghastly, horrible, terrible but it was there. These dead men were men who had worked as coolies in the region, and poverty-stricken townspeople. Before the military flourished, most of them were small traders or porters, and used the money they earned to buy rice and cloth. They were always on the road. After the military triumphed, Songfan's communications with the outside world were completely cut ... only military traffic continued, commerce came to a complete halt. These people had nothing to do. But Songfan's grain was imported. The price of what grain there was on hand flew up. As supplies ran out, there was nowhere left to buy grain. So the coolies were left with nothing to live on, and began to die of starvation. The local people with means felt no compunction to support them. The local commander held discussions with the govern- ment, to lay on relief, or to send them somewhere else as refugees. But the coolies who lived from hand to mouth could not hold off starving until the promised time, but had to give up their pitiful lives earlier. Every day several dozen died in the town.[19]

Interruption of trade meant more than loss of income to merchants; it meant loss of livelihood and then of life to the most vulnerable elements of the commercial world.

Large places could recover from such catastrophes; smaller ones could be destroyed permanently. The blow suffered by a small village near Guangzhou in the summer of 1924 must have been per- manent. A convoy of twenty-three junks, manned by 1,000 of the village's young men, was attacked by the crew of a gunboat. In the attack the village lost several of its young men, all the junks and its entire crop.[20]

The disruption of transport, especially trains, by soldiers also had a strong deterrent effect on trade. Between 1920 and 1930, for example, there was only one year in which the Jing–Han (Peking– Wuhan) line did not suffer a major interruption. Passenger traffic declined, from 4,457,068 in 1924 to 2,063,160 in 1930. Losses of equipment were huge. In 1928, Fengtian troops made off with seventy-six engines (but only seventy-four tenders) and 2,300 pieces of rolling stock in their flight back to Manchuria.[21] No line could run a smooth, reliable service which would encourage goods and passenger traffic while soldiers commandeered trains, smashed up carriages and goods wagons, and let their soldiers ride around for free.

None of the indirect effects of soldier violence and the insecurity it generated can be documented, because it is hard to prove what did not happen. Insecurity is intangible, hard to measure. It is felt, not assessed statistically. In warlord China none of the agencies whose business is insecurity – insurance companies, risk adjusters, investment analysts – operated much beyond the foreign concessions, and the detailed calculations they might have made of the degree of insecurity are therefore not available. It might be possible to develop a counter-factual model of what economic development would have taken place under ideal circumstances. What was clear, however, was that such circumstances did not exist, and that soldiers had a major role in ensuring that they did not.

The spread of violence developed in China a fearful and self-protective mentality. The constant concern with avoiding violence was distracting and self-centred; it focussed attention on self-protection, not on common, collective goals. This inward-turning mentality compounded the damage done by violence, for it reduced the possibility of countering it. Violence became a routine, relished by a few, feared by most. One force which might have broken its rule, the Guomindang, abdicated the responsibility by failing to transform the behaviour of its own military. It was left to the communists to turn Chinese soldiers from inefficient oppressors into servants of the state. They did not outlaw violence, however. Instead, periods like the Cultural Revolution brought in forms of peculiarly horrible violence, whose scars may be even deeper than those inflicted by the soldiers of the Republic.

At the time, the soldiers seemed bad enough. They failed to defend their country against foreign aggression, and indeed their well-known weakness encouraged the Japanese to attack China. They seemed capable only of fighting each other, and of preying on civilians. They *were* capable of better. Cai Tingkai's soldiers, and the handsome Cai himself, became overnight heroes when they fought tenaciously against the Japanese in 1932, at Shanghai. Li Zongren's defence of Taierzhuang in 1938 showed that even soldiers with inferior training were capable of great courage. The sad tale of soldiers was that they were very seldom called upon to show their best, but were usually allowed to show their worst. They were despised by their officers, despised and feared by their countrymen. Only a few warlord or Guomindang commanders realised that if soldiers were treated with respect, they could acquire self-respect, and serve their country. To do this they had to be disciplined and efficient, and they had to stop living off the land. Such a transformation of soldiers was a key element in the success of the communists. The refusal to attempt such a transformation was one of the major reasons for the failure of the Guomindang. It was also the reason why soldiers remained what they had always been in Chinese society, bad iron.

APPENDIX I

CHINESE SOLDIERS –
BIOGRAPHICAL NOTES

BAI CHONGXI 1893–1966. Guangxi general. Trained at Baoding Military Academy. Then local service in Guangxi, followed by long association with Guomindang, interrupted 1929–37. Famous as field commander and strategist. Initiator of comprehensive militia system in native province. One of China's leading Muslims.

CAI TINGKAI 1892–1968. Guomindang's most glamorous commander. Rose from ranks of Guandong provincial forces. Led Chinese defence of Shanghai in 1932, against Japanese invaders; became national hero. Then involved in Fujian Rebellion, 1932. Never again allowed independent command. Joined communists in 1949.

CAO GUN 1862–1938. From humble home in Tianjin, rose through ranks of *Xinjian lujun* to become one of Yuan Shikai's leading subordinates. After Yuan's death, emerged as one of the leaders of the Zhili Clique. Bribed his way to presidency in 1923.

CEN CHUNXUAN 1859–192?. Senior late Qing official. Viceroy of Guandong and Guangxi, 1903–6.

CENG GUOFAN 1811–1872. Leading figure in defence of Qing dynasty against Taiping forces. Outstanding scholar-official. Raised first regional army in China, the Xiang Army, in 1853.

CHEN GUOFU 1892–1951. Leading Guomindang politician. With brother Chen Lifu leader of C.C. Clique. As a child lived in Hunan with his uncle, Chen Qicai, one of first Japanese-trained officers, who raised Hunan New Army.

DENG BAOSAN 1893–1968. Native of Gansu. Served as common soldier in provincial forces, then rose from ranks. A close follower of Feng Yuxiang, followed his rise to power.

FAN SHISHENG ? – ?. Native of Yunnan, a commander in Yunnanese provincial forces until 1925. After defeat in internal struggles, left Yunnan with his army and worked as commander of guest army in various southern provinces. Roving career not hampered by great girth (240 lb) and opium addiction.

FENG YUXIANG 1882–1948. Born into a soldier family in Zhili, enlisted as a child in the Huai Army, then promoted rapidly from ranks. Early revolutionary activity, 1911, Luanzhou Rising. In 1914, conversion to Christianity, often known as 'Christian General' thereafter. Mobile career took him to top of warlord heap, 1924, with establishment of his Guominjun. Uneasy alliance with Guomindang from 1927 culminated in his downfall, 1930. Died mysterious death on Black Sea. Reputation for bluffness, openness and compassion for his men.

HAN FUQU 1890–1938. Early career as common soldier, then close subordinate of Feng Yuxiang. After Feng's downfall, governor of Shandong. Executed for failure to resist Japanese, 1938.

HE LONG 1896–   . Son of leading secret society family in west Hunan. Early bandit/secret society activities, then formal commission in Hunan Army. Brief association with Guomindang ended in 1927, thereafter leading communist commander.

HU JINGYI ? – ?. Adopted son and leading subordinate of Wu Peifu.

HUANG SHAOXIONG 1896–   Guangxi general, early associated with Li Zongren and Bai Chongxi. Broke with them in 1930, thereafter senior civilian appointments from Nanjing government.

LI HONGZHANG 1822–1901. Leading late Qing official. Raised Huai Army (1862), second major regional army. Key role in Qing politics thereafter, as brilliant diplomat and leading moderniser.

LI ZONGREN 1890–1969. Guangxi general. Studied at Guangxi Military Academy, then served in local forces. Established own command in 1920. With Bai Chongxi and Huang Shaoxiong reunified province, then served with Guomindang, 1926–9. Leader of independent Guangxi unit 1937, then renewed, unhappy association with Guomindang. Briefly Vice-President of China in 1949. Strong reputation as field commander after victory against Japanese in 1938 at Taierzhuang. In old age, made triumphal return to China from exile (1965).

LIU RUMING 1896– . Rose from ranks of Zhili Army to become a leading subordinate of Feng Yuxiang.

LIU ZHENHUA 1883– ?. Graduate of traditional examination system. Teacher, then raised own army. Leading military figure in Henan. Subordinate of Wu Peifu. In 1926, transfer to Guomindang.

LONG YUN 1888–1962. Yunnan military leader. Lolo minority origin, strong secret society connections. Provincial governor, 1928–45.

LU RONGTING 1856–1927. Guangxi bandit, incorporated into provincial forces in 1904. Ruler of Guangxi, 1911–20. From 1917–20 also dominated Guangzhou. Ousted from Guangzhou in 1920, soon lost control of Guangxi as well.

LUO BINGHUI 1897–1946. From peasant background in Yunnan, rose through ranks of provincial forces to command level. In 1929 joined communists, thereafter prominent role on Long March and as guerrilla commander in Anti-Japanese War.

PENG DEHUAI 1897–1975. Major communist general. Ran away from home in Hunan as nine-year-old, enlisted in army at seventeen. Rapid rise from ranks of warlord armies. Conversion to communism, mid 1920s, then major military role. Disgraced, 1959. Posthumously rehabilitated, 1979.

QI XIEYUAN 1887–1946. Leading associate of Zhili Clique. Dominant position in Zhejiang until 1927. During Anti-Japanese War collaborated with Japanese, executed in 1946 after Japanese defeat.

SHEN CONGWEN 1903– . Served as common soldier in native west Hunan from 1916 to 1922. Then moved to Beijing and became major writer.

SHI YOUSAN 1882– ?. Leading subordinate of Feng Yuxiang. Betrayed Feng for Nanjing in 1929, then betrayed Nanjing in 1931. Nickname Shi Sanfan – 'Three Times Turncoat'.

WU PEIFU 1874–1939. Leader of Zhili warlord clique. Major military figure in North China, first as subordinate of Yuan Shikai, then in own name. Military career ended in 1926, then into monastery.

YAN XISHAN 1883–1960. Military ruler of Shanxi, 1912–49. Promoter of provincial independence and provincial improvement.

YANG XIMIN ? – ?. Yunnan general. Commander of Yunnan troops on Guangzhou, 1922–4. Known for corruption and veniality.

YUAN SHIKAI 1859–1916. Founder of China's modern armies. Second president of Republic of China, 1912–16.

ZHANG GUOTAO 1897–1980. Son of Jiangxi gentry family, then founding member of C.C.P. Leader of Oyuwan Soviet, 1929–32, then of West Sichuan Soviet, 1932–35. Subsequently broke with C.C.P.

ZHANG ZONGCHANG 1881–1932. Migrated from Shandong to Manchuria as child, there became bandit. Went into regular army in 1912, rose to dominance in North China. Military career of startling brutality ended 1928. Assassinated 1932.

ZHANG ZUOLIN 1873–1928. Early career as militiaman/bandit in Manchuria led to formal military career. Ruled Manchuria 1919–28. Close associate of Japanese, but still assassinated by them.

ZHU ZHIXIN 1885–1920 Leading associate of Sun Yatsen. Early classical education, then study in Japan. Revolutionary activist and theorist, also military commander. Killed in battle in 1920.

APPENDIX 2

'YOUNGER BROTHER' ('DIDI')

In China as elsewhere wild young men who had gone beyond their family's ability to control were prime candidates for the army. Rowdiness was not considered a natural part of youth, and the bad behaviour of a boy was a source of shame to his family, and to himself. Zhou Wen's story 'Younger brother' ('Didi') shows this process of growing shame and anger. Zhou himself went into the army at a very young age, when his widowed mother was no longer able to support him. He also had a younger brother who died in the army, so it is probable that this story is strongly autobiographical. Zhou never made a great name as a writer, though his stories are vivid and moving. His first stories were published in the early 1930s, before he joined the communists in Yanan in 1936. He died about 1950. This story is translated from *Fuzi zhi jian*, Shanghai, 1934, pp. 1–10.

Didi [younger brother] – he left this world more than a year ago. I still can't decide whether his death was his blessing or his misfortune. But when I have some spare moments, in the midst of all my business, or when I lie awake with my eyes wide open at night, his simple face comes into my mind, I seem to hear the word 'gege' [elder brother] beside my ear, and his dead body, with the flesh and blood all blurred, seems to be there before my eyes. It hurts, but I want to use this pain to fix some memories which I don't want to forget.

When Didi was little, he was very naughty. He never seemed to understand that he should be starting to get an education. When our father died he was three* and of course he did not understand the difficulties that the family was in. But as time went on, my mother's plans each year at the New Year were all for me; all he could do was

* In traditional China, a child was one year old at birth: '3' here probably means '2' according to Western counting. The same applies to all other ages quoted here.

open his innocent eyes wide, as if he were listening to people talking about outside affairs which had nothing to do with him. But by the time he was ten, he really should have started to go to school.

My mother had already started to spit blood, but she was still determined to go on fighting against the bullying of my uncles, her husband's brothers. She carried on the small shop my father had left, and put great effort into keeping up appearances in front of our relations and friends. All of this was for us. What she hoped was that her sons would win credit for her. So her life went on. Every year, especially towards the end of the year, she had to go round from place to place getting money for our schooling together. No, I should say it was really only for me. Borrowing money was very difficult. Every time she went up to someone's shop counter with her meek eyes cast down, all she could think was: let's get the money for the elder one first. So Didi was left aside.

Didi had a tough body, and his face, legs and arms were all tanned. He was small, but he had a fierce temper, and as soon as he set eyes on someone, he opened his huge black eyes wide. I very seldom saw him when I came out of school each afternoon; it was only in the evening, when my mother lit a vegetable oil lamp for me to do my homework by that he came home, with a bloody nose and a bruised face. Sometimes there were long scratches on his face. Of course my mother would cuff him round the ears too, and put him over the bench and tan his behind. Even before the stick hit him, he started to screech, but when the beating was over a look of bitterness and truculence shone out from his dark face. It always finished with my mother wiping the tears from her eyes with her long sleeves. But my mother only really sobbed when my father died; she banged her head against his coffin in her grief. She had to put up with the trouble-making of my uncles; they started rumours against her among the neighbours. Now she could only sob quietly, looking stealthily out of the window while she was crying to see whether there were any prying eyes there. Her mind was pulled this way and that over her various preoccupations: she was afraid that her elder son would not concentrate; she was furious about her younger son letting her down; she was afraid that the neighbours would hear; and she was worried about the business in the shop. When she heard the clerks quarrelling with a customer, she dried her tears, put on a casual expression, and hobbled off on her bound feet to calm things down.

But this did not make Didi any better. He sat at the table twisting his clothes and biting his lips. My mother said:

'Xiao Tian, eat up.'

No answer.

'Come on, eat up.'

Still no answer. He clenched his lips.

'You're asking for another beating.'

But he still didn't reply.

Only when our grandfather came in, smoking his pipe, talking with a throaty growl, did Didi slink out like a rat. When mother saw our grandfather coming, she masked her tears with a smile of welcome. Grandfather had believed the rumours that my uncles spread about my mother, and had cursed her bitterly. He stamped his foot now, and swore at her:

'You shameless woman. Go back to your own family. You have no right to soil our family's good name.'

Didi was afraid of him. After he had slipped out of the room, he made a noise like a gun going off outside the window, and then ran off to practise his fighting with some of his wild friends. He was quite blatant about his bad behaviour.

One day, one of the clerks was caught cheating my mother. He had been putting money from things he had sold straight into his own pocket. He would not admit what he had done, just wanted to pack his things and leave at once. He seemed to be saying: 'If it wasn't for me, how would you, this widow, have managed to keep going until now?'

In the middle of her fury, Didi happened to come home, back from some nefarious activity elsewhere. The beating he got from her was fiercer than ever. She yelled as she beat him: 'Why are you such a disappointment?'

'Ow, ow, ow.'

'How are you ever going to grow up?'

'Ow, ow, ow.'

'How are you . . .'

'Ow, ow, ow.'

The people who were listening all had a good laugh. The more my mother beat him, the harder she hit. Didi's cries stopped, and the only sound was the stick hitting his behind.

This time, when my mother finally came out of the house, there was no sign of Didi. By evening the whole house was in a state of alarm, and everyone went out with flares to look for him. My mother was so worried that she was white in the face, almost mad with agitation. The neighbours' faces were full of pleasure at her misery, as if they felt that the Widow Tian had brought retribution on herself. Bit by bit they increased the pressure on her.

'Has he run away?'

'Yes.'

'Why did he run away?'

'Humph! He just went.'

Luckily my mother did not collapse when she overheard these words. She told me as she sobbed that she shouldn't have beaten him unjustly. After a lot of upset, he was found the next morning, behind the door of the main hall of our aunt's house. He was dragged home. After this people gave him the nickname 'savage'.

Didi actually was rather savage. He was always jeering at me because I had been made the heir of my oldest aunt. When Didi saw me smiling after he had got into trouble he would shout roughly at me:

'Why don't you go to your own home?'

Although I felt insulted, all I could do was let him get away with it; I was frightened that he would use his tough fists against my puny body.

'Ah, ah, you're shameless. You eat food from another family. You're well off. Those new clothes should belong to my family!'

When he talked like that, I felt like taking the clothes off at once, and running off to my aunt's house in a fit of pique. But my mother held me back. She told me not to take any notice of what he said. She said that I was a boy whom everbody liked, while he was a 'savage'.

Sometimes Didi-the-Savage was very useful to me. Once, not far from our gate, a boy from our school started to bully me. Red in the face with fury, I put up my fists, but the boy was not the least bit scared, and kept on standing truculently in front of me, making all the people standing round laugh. Didi rushed over brandishing a steel bar, part of a steel-yard. We could all hear the metal fixtures on it clanking as he came. The boy who was bullying me jumped out of his skin, and dashed away. Didi ran after him a little way. Naturally the people standing round laughed again, but this time the laughter had quite a different note.

Sometimes when my mother was at her wits end she would stop sewing, and with a distant look in her eye would say quietly to herself:

'The fortune teller says I still have ten years to live. One of my sons will be in the literary world, one in the military. Ten years...'

Although she said ten years, the little smile at the corners of my mother's mouth seemed to say that it wouldn't necessarily work out like that. By this time she felt that she really had to get Didi into school. She wanted to lock him up in school, and then sit back and wait for the ten years to pass. Because of a lack of money, Didi and I had to go to different schools; he went with ragged local children. Within a year I noticed that he had broken the back of the Three Character Classic. Only God knew how the teacher in his school taught, or how the children studied. When I came home for the summer holidays from my school in another county, my mother told me that the teacher smoked opium, and that Didi was often brought back dripping from the little river [where he had been playing truant].

Later on, our life got worse and worse by the day. It was almost impossible to keep the shop going. My mother made me leave school; I was to go to a relation who was an army officer. As for Didi, he was now fourteen; the only thing to do with him was to keep him at school for another two years, until he could manage the shop, and take over from my mother.

While my mother and I were talking these things over, Didi was standing silently by the door. Then he went away without a word, off to play cards and gamble. Because it was the New Year, my mother didn't stop him. Later I asked him: 'Didi, what school do you want to go to this year?' His reply was: 'Don't bother about me.' He glared at me and left the house. After that the shop assistants started to tease him:

'Xiao Tian – You go on playing cards. Your big brother wants to be an officer.'

Didi threw down his cards, narrowed his eyes and said:

'Don't put your money on it. Him! Be an officer! Up yours.'

'Well, *you* certainly don't behave like someone who is going to be an officer.'

'Beat it!'

My mother suddenly grabbed a plank and rushed over.

'I don't believe it! You mustn't fight at New Year. If you want to have a row, wait until your mother has closed her eyes.'

Didi was so angry that his eyes were popping out of his head. He turned on Wang Er who was sitting beside him, tossed down his cards and disappeared like a puff of smoke.

A day later, one of the shop assistants told my mother that he had heard Wang Er and Didi talking secretly about running away. So my mother quickly went and opened the chest, to see that the money was all there; there was nothing missing. She ran and got a padlock and locked it. She thought that if he had no money he would not dare run away. Anyhow, he who had never been away from home would never be able to find the road with Wang Er. She had taken her precautions and that was it.

Who would have thought that the day before the one that my mother had chosen as a good day for me to leave on my journey Wang Er's mother would come running over to ask if we had seen her son? Only then did my mother discover that Didi was missing. She got very upset. Everyone was sent out to search for him again. Mother went and looked in the chest again. It was fine. So was the money. Nothing had been moved. Mother clasped the sweaty clothes that Didi had worn the day before and started to cry. She wept because she said she should not have neglected his education; she said that she hadn't brought him up well. She had not even made him any decent clothes. He had not even chosen a lucky day to leave home, had not taken any money with him.

'I should have treated him fairly', she sobbed out.

In the midst of her despair, all she could hope was that he had gone off to our relation. She got some of his clothes together, and put them in my trunk. She even wrapped up some of his favourite biscuits and put them in too, with some sweets.

'If you see your brother, give them to him, and tell him not to forget his mother.'

As soon as she got that far, she started to sob again, and her tears dripped down into the tube of sweets.

'How am I going to go on? Before you came home, he said to me, "Ma, you're old and suffering, next year I'll look after the shop for you." I said ... then he said, "don't make any clothes for me, I can wear my brother's" ... and then I find he was deceiving me, running off like this! He threw away so many chances. How am I...?'

Mother was overwhelmed by her tears and couldn't get any more out. I stood helplessly beside her.

'Mama, Didi can't have disappeared. He must have gone there. I don't want to go by sedan chair. I'll walk.'

Mother struggled to get her eyes open. She looked at me. Her lips moved with great emotion.

'No,' she said, 'the sedan chair is already booked. Go in it. You mustn't give people a chance to laugh at us. You must go in the chair, even if your mother has to eat gruel. Just so long as you do well away from home, and make careers, and come back with some money. Just remember to tell your brother not to forget his mother...'

I left home in the sedan chair, under the admiring eyes of several people. When I got to my relations, they did in fact tell me that Didi had already arrived. At first they had wanted to send him home at once, but he absolutely refused. He said he would do any kind of work. So in the end they let him stay there as an ordinary soldier.

(The story goes on to describe the difficult relations between the two brothers in the army, one a cadet officer, the other an ordinary soldier. It ends with the death of the younger brother in battle.)

APPENDIX 3

REPORTS OF MUTINIES

The military history of warlord China was punctuated by mutinies. One of the most dramatic took place in Beijing not long after the establishment of the new Republic in early 1912. The new (second) president of the Republic, Yuan Shikai [Yuan Shih-k'ai] was unable to prevent his own troops from the 3rd Division from mutinying, and, even though the mutiny was soon put down, the unfavourable impression created by a mutiny in the capital greatly weakened Yuan's ability to deal with foreign pressure. These reports, printed in the Shanghai newspaper *North China Herald* on 9 March 1912, give some idea of what went on.

THE MUTINY IN PEKING

President's Message of Regret   Peking, 1 March. Yuan Shih-kai has issued a communiqué to the foreign missionaries, merchants and other residents: 'The unexpected disturbance has filled me with sorrow. One of my chief duties is to preserve order in the capital. Hitherto I have been uniformly successful. Unto you, strangers in a strange land, I wish particularly to convey my sincere regret. Every measure of precaution is now taken to prevent recurrence.'

The vicinity of the Legation is quiet. There is a fire near the North Gate and some disant shooting. Fifteen hundred mutineers commandeered a train early this morning and departed for Honan.

Our own correspondent

Terrible Scenes   Peking, 1 March. The outbreak began in the 3rd Division quartered near Yuan Shi-kai's headquarters.

After firing many volleys, numerous large bands streamed off in various directions looting systematically, principally gold and silver art curios from the pawnshops, and shooting off their rifles to intimidate the inmates. In several instances shopkeepers who did not promptly hand over their valuables were roughly handled. Some were shot or bayoneted, as the soldiers carried rifles and bayonets and some hundred rounds of ammunition. One party operated near Dr G. E. Morrison's house. They set light to a pawnshop. The flames spread rapidly, causing a gigantic conflagration. It was a weird scene, under the vivid glare, some mutineers shooting into the fires, others rushing in gangs from shop to shop, breaking in doors and smashing furniture and staggering off with their loot.

In the Glare of the Fire

Hundreds of the inmates were seen in the smoky glare escaping over the roofs of the houses in terror-stricken parties.

Some foreign troops forming a striking contrast to the excited looters passed through their midst unmolested, and brought in foreigners to the Legation area. In the vicinity of the Hatamen Road tremendous looting and burnings took place. Outside the Chienmen thousands looted for hours. The orderly troops were not able to restore order. Many joined the looters as also did the police and thousands of coolies and loafers.

At one in the morning there were seven fires burning, three covering large areas, but the shooting was dwindling owing to the expenditure of ammunition and exhaustion of the mutineers, hundreds of whom, leading ponies loaded with spoil, were leaving the city. The reflection from the golden roofs of the Forbidden City was gorgeous. Many figures on it could be discerned, presumably eunuchs watching the fires but not knowing the cause, for the outbreak was a complete surprise to the Government, the Legations and others.

At two in the morning the looters probably totalled 10,000 and efforts to suppress them had ceased. The rattle of musketry was heard periodically until morning, momentarily growing more distant as the operations widended.

Control Reappearing

Chang Wei-te's troops outside the Hatamen partially controlled the looters and today they were brought inside for patrol work. But looting on the outskirts continues though the majority of the looters have left the city. A few shells were fired from the East Gate and one dropped in the quarters of the American guard but did no damage.

Foreigners were not injured. Yuan Shih-kai and the more prominent leaders are safe. Ten looters were captured and executed this morning. Some apprehensions are felt for what may happen to-night.

Our own correspondent

A month later another major mutiny broke out in Nanjing [Nanking], the temporary capital of the Republic at the time of its establishment, and the major city of the lower Yangzi Valley. This account, from a rather adventurous foreign resident, appeared in the *North China Herald* for 20 April 1912.

THE MUTINY

There was nothing in the air on Friday night to suggest that the peace was to be disturbed. The exhibition buildings, a hundred yards away from my house, were dead quiet and there was no indication that they were filled with soldiers plotting mischief. At a quarter past twelve I was roused by the noise of two shots that reverberated loud and clear in the still air. Further shooting followed immediately and then the sound of many voices floated insistently across from the barracks. In the pitch black night the flashing of the rifle was plainly visible and the noise of the voices was steadily rising into a chorus of yells and shouts. It was clear that something unusual was happening. The flashing of the rifles occurred at two points and suggested that fighting between different sections of the troops in the city was about to take place, and that the soldiers after trouble with their officers were marching off to begin their dangerous work.

I tumbled into my clothes and sallied out into the darkness, where I was joined by a foreign friend living near. We walked down the Maloo in the direction of the Drum Tower whence sounds of continuous shooting and shouting proceded. In the distance a brilliant reflection in the sky showed that looting had been preceded in the orthodox manner by the raising of fire. There was some reason for nervousness as shooting both before and behind us was constant. It took us a little time to appreciate that the soldiers were only firing in the air to defend themselves from evil spirits. Our advance therefore was conducted with some trepidation even though there was no danger except from stray bullets. We met a succession of parties bringing back loot. This was loaded either in rickshas or slung on poles and rifles. The men were very excited and shouted and talked among themselves, every now and then discharging their rifles. This they seemed to do out of nervousness, and with no particular regard for direction. At last we came to a point only 200 yards away from the Drum Tower, where we met a rush of returning looters and were nearly knocked down by them. One man was most emphatic in warning us not to proceed, and as the firing in front was heavy and continuous and the yelling decidedly blood-curdling, we decided to halt.

We retraced our steps to the Bureau of Foreign Affairs, a foreign building standing inside a large wall, where we found the Director and the whole of the staff freshly risen out of bed and greatly agitated by the firing outside. As foreigners we were comparatively safe from attack, but as Chinese they were liable to any kind of treatment at the hands of the soldiers. The firing which continually recurred at their very door was peculiarly alarming but I explained to them that this had very little significance, as the soldiers fired only into the air. I shall never forget the solemnity with which one young official sententiously uttered: 'They ought not to do that; it is very disturbing to the public mind.' Our opinion that the soldiers were only out for loot, however, restored confidence, and after endless telephoning we learnt that troops were looting the Pehmenchiao [Beimenqiao] district immediately to the south of the Drum Tower. We soon had the satisfaction of hearing that a large force was under orders to suppress the mutineers. So far as we could discover only the soldiers at the Exhibition and at one small barracks beside the Drum Tower were in revolt, so that with a great majority of the large garrison still obedient, the task of restoring order did not promise difficulty.

After a strenuous night spent in the Bureau of Foreign Affairs, in the genial company of Mr Wan and his staff, we left at the first sign of dawn and walked towards the Drum Tower. Crowds of looters were still pouring back laden with booty of the most heterogeneous character. None of it seemed very valuable, bedding, enamelled dishes, crockery and so forth, obviously the household goods of poor people. The firing of rifles was still a prominent feature of the proceedings. We got all the emotion we wanted in that walk, and would have gladly bolted back if to do that had been safer than to go forward. The soldiers continued to show great excitement, and brushed past us roughly as if their night of plundering had made them reckless of consequences.

Arrived at the village surrounding the Drum Tower, we found the houses gutted and the despoiled inhabitants standing disconsolately about. The Tower had apparently been the centre of disturbance, for the revolted soldiers had kept up a chorus of yelling all night, accompanied by continuous shooting. For residents in the neighbourhood had been particularly alarmed by the constant shouting of dah! dah! dah! (kill! kill! kill!) and without accurate knowledge of what was happening had some reason for fearing that the excitement might take an anti-foreign direction. They had not been molested in any way, however.

While we were having a welcome cup of tea, the intermittent firing increased considerably, and we wondered what the reason was until we saw the slopes of the Drum Tower suddenly invaded by crowds of soldiers. These with loud shouting rushed forward and took up positions on the sky-line. We quickly ran out and joined them and found them to be the Cantonese troops ordered out during the night to suppress the mutinied troops. They had marched from the southern part of the town and had cleared the Pehmenchiao street as they advanced. This street goes south from the Drum Tower about half a mile from which there is a thickly inhabited part of the city. Here the principal looting had occurred, and many of the mutineers were caught red-handed and shot down as they ran. We afterwards went out and saw many dead lying in the lanes and field, evidently men who had tried to escape from the oncoming troops.

Simultaneously with the advance from the south, which drove the looters back upon their barracks, other forces drove the mutinied troops back upon their barracks from other directions, with the result that between six and seven in the morning, the two revolted regiments were corralled in the exhibition buildings. The surrounding troops poured a few volleys into them, and after a little ineffective return fire, the mutineers surrendered.

. . .

Coming to the question of the reason of the rising, there is little doubt that the immediate cause was the fact that the soldiers had received no pay either in March or April... The troops principally concerned were two regiments of two battalions each, of Kiangsi [Jiangxi] men. A battalion and a half of these were actively concerned. Two battalions who had been deprived of their ammunition a month before, on account of mutinous behaviour, were not engaged, though their officers had great difficulty in restraining them. A certain number of Chekiang [Zhejiang] troops stationed in the exhibition barracks are reported to have joined in, as well as some Hunanese stationed elsewhere. The total number involved was probably not more than 1,200 to 1,300. Of the men actually caught with loot upon them it is stated by witnesses that nearly a hundred have been beheaded. Nearly another hundred were shot down during the advance of the Cantonese troops, and in the attacks on the barracks. Some casualties occurred among citizens, but the number is insignificant.

APPENDIX 4

'IN THE ARMY'

Routine, savage beatings were the norm in most Chinese military units. Officers saw beating not only as a punishment for offenders but also as a means of warning other potential offenders off. For this reason beatings were usually administered in public. The author of this short story, only the first part of which is translated here, is Xiao Jun, a well-known writer of the 1930s and 1940s. Xiao Jun was born in Manchuria in 1908. He went into the army in 1925, first as a common soldier, though he was later promoted to officer. After the Japanese invasion of Manchuria in 1931, he left the regular army and became an anti-Japanese guerrilla. In 1934 he fled to Shanghai, where his most famous book, *Village in August*, was published the same year. He was a protégé of China's greatest modern writer, Lu Xun, but this relationship was not enough to prevent him later on from being attacked by the Communist literary watchdogs as an 'anti-proletarian writer'. These attacks ended the literary career of a writer whose concern for the sufferings of ordinary Chinese was deeply felt and passionately expressed. This translation is taken from *Yang*, Hong Kong, 1952, pp 93-100.

1935

A man was being beaten again.

Two – three – four ... five, six, seven, eight, ten, two ... three ... four ... five, six, seven, eight, twenty ... thirty ... fifty ... one hundred ...

When the count reached five hundred, the sound of wood and flesh smacking together, and the anguished curses and screams which followed it, finally stopped. During the last hundred of the count, the sound of the rod rising and falling had slowed down; the strokes were still not light, but there were fewer really heavy strokes – in a normal beating in the army things slowed down like this.

'Change, change men ... stinking son-of-a-bitch, stinking so-and-so ...'

The rod clattered on the bricks of the path, with a metallic ring. I knew that the man who was taking over was a powerful 'punisher', and my ears pricked up again.

Two, three, four ... five, six, seven, eight ... ten, twenty ... seventy ... the count reached one hundred again.

'Stinking son-of-a-bitch ... I want you to give his itches a good scratching ... itches'.

A sound – apparently the sound of a man's hand striking somewhere on a face. I couldn't decide who it had struck. Judging from the sound, the man who was doing the striking had already used up all his strength – it was flat, satiated.

The sound of flesh and wood meeting also seemed flat and satiated. It didn't sound as resounding as before; then it had a sing-song, rising and falling sound of 'punishment' in it. Now it was flat, satiated ... echoing, a confused echo. I jumped down from my bed and shoved my hands deep into my trouser pockets. My boots with spurs on them struck the ground with a jangle. A voice which seemed to have been strangled for a long while faltered out, as if from a tiny crack which would barely let breath through:

'Commander ... let ... let ... my leg ...'

The last word sounded like a grain of coarse sand with no rough edges to it, sinking silently into a calm sea. Feebly, sinking away, like a spider's web blown away by a slight gust of wind ...

The sound of the rod started up again as before, each time as if it were striking immobile flesh, except that sometimes you could hear the wood and flesh grating together.

I went out of my room; the little iron rings on the spurs of my riding boots jangled softly as I walked.

The weather was good; it was spring, the season that made men feel sleepy. In front of the battalion headquarters the lilacs were in full bloom, purple mixed with white. The scent wafted over by the breeze was also like a colour – purple or white.

The face of the man with his head pushed down was flushed red; he seemed to be right at the end of his strength. The head which had been trying to sway, to cry out, was now sleeping peacefully on the ground, mired in its own snot and saliva. As for the man whose job it was to mark time by stamping his feet, his hands were no longer clapping in unison, and his stamping feet had started to slacken. Only the man who was holding his [the victim's] legs still kneaded the ground mechanically with his knees, holding the man down by his ankles.

His trousers were drawn down, and his fresh blood stained his yellow skin ... the sunlight shone down from the pale blue sky, everything was peaceful ... tranquil ...

'Get some water ...'

A douche of icy water poured down on to his head, and from the icy water a sound groaned out.

Commander Zhao, and the deputy officer of the battalion, were both there. The red sash of the duty officer was draped ostentatiously over the shoulders of Commander Zhao, which were not very well suited to wear it – mainly because he was so skinny that he was almost invisible; the deputy officer on the other hand was a fierce looking fellow.

We went through the normal ceremony.

'Help him up ... the game's not over yet.'

Commander Zhao's lips looked ever more like those of an old woman: extremely thin, tight, not the colour of flesh, or of blood, but like worn-out leather. Both hands grasped the handle of the cane, and pounded it on the bricks of the path. Nothing about the cane suited him – not the length, the weight, the thickness ... or the clear black colour. He was obviously beside himself with rage. Every time he stamped his foot on the bricks like a child, his spurs jangled. His boots were totally Japanese in style, with narrow upper parts; they were a very shiny black, which hit your eyes like a mirror.

Some people were holding Wang the Beard up, getting him to walk up and down the courtyard ... his beard was full of mud, his puttees had already come unravelled before the beating started. His eyes, no longer young, were filled with water or with tears – at any rate they were blurred. His little red nose, which normally seemed sharp, was smeared with mud, and there was mud on his forehead.

'All right ... you stinking grub ... if we don't do your legs we can't finish. Bring him back ... put him down on his front.'

The deputy officer's eyes caught mine. I could see from his eyes that he was a timid man, someone who did not dare to interfere.

'Give it to him!'

The soldiers saluted. Wang the Beard was being supported

131

between two men, his head hanging down. His scabby scalp glistened in the sun.

'It's not right ... right ... right ... why don't you stop a bit earlier?'

The black bags under the commander's eyes puffed up; the whites of his eyes were bluish.

'Give it to him!'

'You ... you ... you're going to do it to me?'

The response was the stamping of the commander's foot and the pounding of the cane; they stirred up the dust a little. The scent of the lilacs, mixed with the dust, floated over into my nostrils.

He was spread-eagled on the ground as before, with four men stationed round his body as before. The man holding him round the waist gave a twist of his wrists ... his trousers slipped reluctantly, with difficulty down the yellow thighs stained with blood, down to their original position. The colour of the blood was no longer as fresh, it was purplish in the places where it had already soaked through his trousers. Where it had started to flow again it was no different than before. It seemed paler, but still red.

'Comm .. ander ... sir ... I can't ... go on ...'

The sound came out like sand ... like a cobweb ... sinking; it broke off ... but every time the cane came down, you had to listen to the moans as well as the sound of flesh and bone being split open ... the groans that came with that sound. Part of the cane was coated with red lacquer, but its colour did not blend in with the colour of human blood!

Afterwards another douche of icy water was poured over Wang the Beard's head, and another two men hauled him up from the ground and walked him back and forth. His eyes were even more blurred; the little red nose which used to look sharp and the little beard which was normally neat and looked like copper wire both had a lot more mud on them. On parts of the face, behind the mud, there were streaks of blood and mud mixed together, flowing and dripping down; his face had got so close to the earth that it had been scratched.

The deputy commander's eyes met mine again – his hulking body did not fit well with his rodent eyes.

Only when Commander Zhao discovered that there were spots of the old soldier's blood on his gleaming boots did he toss the cane on to the brick-paved path – it made another metallic clang.

'Take him away ... take him ...'

They didn't take him, they dragged him.

'You ... you ... don't dare ...'

'I won't dare do it again! Commander, sir!' Although the voice was so faint that it was scarcely audible, the whole courtyard apparently heard it clearly. The door of every barrack, the upper open parts of every window were full of men in grey, all standing stunned like leaden figures.

'Be careful of your legs ... legs ... take him away.'

Usually in the armies when officers had men beaten they were not stingy afterwards, and gave out some money for wine, for straw paper [for bandages] and for ointment. This showed the officer's decency, showed that he understood the ways of soldiers. This was how the soldiers could feel the compassion [of their officers]. But today as an exception to the rule Commander Zhao did not do it. From the distance someone called out:

'His legs are all cut up. Aren't you going to give some money for straw paper? Do you understand how we do things?'

Where did the voice come from? Commander Zhao couldn't find out. It seemed to come from every window, no, from every man.

Commander Zhao walked off without any farewell. He clutched the red sash of the duty officer, which shone vividly, and walked out of the camp. Through the gate I could see the Sungari River, more than a thousand metres away, the river water calm and still, as if it had stopped flowing.

The deputy commander's eyes started to move in their monkey sockets; his eyebrows started to move with them, as he walked along the path. Finally he stopped and looked out of the gate, apparently listening. The voice from the place outside the walls where the horses were tethered seemed to be Commander Zhao's; right behind the voice two grooms came through the gate. In Commander Zhao's hand was a horse-whip.

I recognised the two grooms. They were two fellows, Qiong Bao and Lao Cao, who often went drinking with Wang the Beard.

'What's going on now?' I asked the deputy commander.

'What ... who knows?'

It soon became clear. A horse's harness had not been put on properly, and the horse had lain down on the ground. This was the duty officer's responsibility.

This time Commander Zhao did not want to use the cane, so he just made Qiong Bao and Lao Cao kneel on the path, and flogged them with the horse-whip, on their backs.

Qiong Bao was young, and he was trying to give reasons. But Commander Zhao never listened to reasons. In the army only the officers had reasons. In the army it was like this: there was obedience of orders; there was no questioning of reasons. The first day I entered the army, the commander's first words to me were on those lines. He also said: 'An officer can burst your brains out without giving a reason, and you still can't ask for a reason. The only thing is obedience.'

It was true. If your head was hacked off, the reason that counted was all on the officer's side. With your head off, you couldn't ask for a reason anyhow. But now I was an officer myself, and on my feet were boots with spurs. These words were now even more real, and even more important for me to remember.

'AS THE BANDITS DO THINGS'

There was often little to choose for the ordinary peasants of China between bandit or soldier control. This account from an itinerating missionary B. G. Parsons illustrates the misery of villages regularly visited by the two types of armed men. This account was published in the *Chinese Recorder* for 1924, 197-8.

An experience we had in a village called Liang-a, Fukien [Fujian] will give an idea of some of the present difficulties. We found the village in the hands of bandits; a bandit sentry, posted on the bridge leading to the village, gave us a most correct salute as we passed! This was about midday; we put up at the house of a Christian school-master and having had tiffin my wife and I were unpacking our bedding when suddenly we were startled by rifle shots close at hand. Looking out of the window we saw several bandits running for all they were worth and men who had been working in the fields hasten-ing to take cover. The people of the house begged us to come down, as the upstairs room in which we were lodged had only a thin outside partition of wood and they were afraid of stray bullets coming through! To relieve their fears we did so, though we much wanted to view the battle. Not that there was anything of a fight, for, as usually happens on these occasions, the attacking party of soldiers, instead of surrounding the place, came in from one side and gave timely warning of their approach by letting off their guns at long range, almost before they caught sight of a bandit to shoot at! The bandits took the hint and ran out of the village on the opposite side and made for the hills as fast as their legs would carry them! Net result of this round up: a young man of the village killed by accident and one bandit shot, I do not know whether by accident or not! The rest got away, two boys tending cows outside the village caused their parents grave anxiety by not returning home that night; but they turned up next morning, having fled to a neighbouring village when the fight started. But what does it mean for the villagers? For weeks they had the bandits living on them and extorting money from those who were better off; out go the bandits only to give place to the soldiers who will billet themselves on these poor long-suffering people for a further week or two while they recover from their 'fight', and then they will depart and leave the place open to the bandits once more. And so it goes on, they told me, month after month and they are never left in peace for long; with the people living under conditions of this sort it is by no means an easy task to build up and extend the Church.

'THE MURDERER'

Sha Ting is the pen name of Yang Chengfang, born in Sichuan in 1905. As a young man he spent several years in the army, before becoming a writer in 1931. He was left-wing rather than communist, a disciple of Lu Xun, and a passionate advocate of the down-trodden. His style tends to be melodramatic and tear-jerking, in tune with the literary style of the time. But the fate of men who were seized by the army as porters was so grim that this story should not be seen as unusually tragic. Only the execution of one brother by another should be put down to artistic licence. This translation is taken from *Sha Ting xuanji*, Hong Kong, 1956, pp. 91–100.

May 1935

Like a mangy dog, the broken-legged soldier waited in the River God's temple for his last days to come. This temple had been built on the ridge at the entrance to the gully at Mujiagou. It was only about six metres square, with white walls and black tiles; it looked like a blockhouse. The ridge stretched for two or three miles, and because it had some placer gold deposits, there had once been a gold rush there; that was when the temple had been built. But now, looking out from the door of the temple, there was not a sign of life, nor could you even hear the sound of a hoe cultivating the earth. All that was left was a stretch of dead silence, and the caved-in entrance to the mine, with no buildings left.

When he came back from the battlefield, the broken-legged soldier had been put straight out of the house by his father, because the old fellow had already heard the story of the death of his second son. He cursed him crudely, refused to believe what his son swore was true, and had no pity for the wound which had crippled him. He treated him as if he was the murderer of his younger brother. The only person who had any sympathy for this pitiful person was his mother.

She gave him food in secret, and kept on at her old man to try and bring him round. But while she waited for her son to eat the food, the old woman could not help sighing all the time, and haltingly coming out with words which hurt him deeply. So one afternoon he suddenly stopped chewing, and leaning back against the wall cried out:

'Say it! You think I killed him.'

Then he started to weep, and after that he would not eat the bitter-tasting food. He started his life as a beggar.

Now the broken-legged soldier had been completely forgotten by his family. But a few years ago he had been an important member of the family, although his position in the family was lower than his brother's. This brother was a young man of twenty-two or twenty-three. He had had a few years at an old-fashioned school, and since his marriage he had done very little farm work. Instead he spent most of his time studying medicine with his father-in-law. His father's hopes for the future doctor were very great, because the losses he had suffered in the trade in firewood and other forest products had broken his self-confidence, and at the same time he knew that being a peasant was something you could never escape from. Every day after he had had some drink he bemoaned his fate. The woodseller had two other sons, both very young, so all the farm work fell on the shoulders of the broken-legged soldier. He was very good at manual work, and only seemed to be interested in manual work. If he had nothing to do for a while, he would fall asleep in the middle of the day; he just sat still in one place, without making a sound, without even smiling. Because of his good nature, this disciple of good deeds who seemed to be stuck in a rut was called the 'dolt'. But very few people called him that to his face because there was still something honest about him.

One night in the spring of 1925, the broken-legged soldier's wife died after a hard labour. This was the first pregnancy since they had been married several years before. The old fellow started cursing, and complaining that he had no spare money floating around to waste. But the next day he got some money together and told the broken-legged soldier to arrange his wife's funeral. Since he had never had any faith in his intelligence, he told the doctor to go in to town with him. The two brothers arranged the important business very quickly. They ordered a simple coffin, and hired two Daoist priests. All that was left was to buy various things like oil and wine. The broken-legged soldier could do these things on his own, so at the door of the priests' house the doctor arranged a meeting place with him and then turned and ran off to the government office, to have a look at the public announcements. The broken-legged soldier followed suit and went off to the bustling market-place. But at the crossroads beneath the drum tower he was grabbed by some irregular soldiers who were press-ganging porters.

'Master, someone has died in my family.' He started to struggle with them.

'Don't move.'

'Truly – the dead person is still laid out in the house. Go and ask.'

But these grey-clad friends seemed to have no desire to find out if what he said were true or not. They roped him together with a bunch of other men from the country and drove him off to the place where the porters were being corralled. It was a temple with crimson pillars. In the main hall twenty or thirty peasants were already sitting, his brother amongst them. The young man was sitting with his arms round his knees; when he looked up his whole face was full of fury. As the broken-legged soldier saw him, he couldn't help being startled, because up till then he had only been thinking of the money he had lost, of his dead wife, and of the anger of his old man.

The broken-legged soldier was silent for a while, then he sighed and said: 'So you were grabbed too?'

His brother suddenly recognised him, but only glared at him and then looked away.

They were held in captivity for two months, and then they set out [on a campaign] with the garrison army. They served together under a company commander. The work was light, because the person who rode in the litter they carried was a slight young maidservant. On the road the two brothers were very considerate of each other; the anger of the time when they were arrested seemed to have passed. They were only trying to work out how to get home. But once they got to the place they were going they were tied up again. Someone said they were going to get some wages. The episodes of press-ganging porters in Sichuan were always strange, and so when they got over their astonishment they started to make all kinds of vivid guesses.

One evening after supper they were all still holding their rice bowls and talking about this windfall, wondering whether it was real or not, trying to work out how much they would get. The doctor said nothing at first, but then he banged his chopsticks and broke in to what the others were saying:

'Wages!', the doctor cried out full of derision, 'I just want them to let me go sooner.'

Then the broken-legged soldier sighed.

'You're right', he said gloomily, 'I'm afraid they're going to make us stay on as soldiers.'

'Where did you hear that? You're talking rubbish.' The doctor started to get angry.

'Talking rubbish? That fellow told me just now . . .'

Before he'd finished speaking, his brother flung aside his chopsticks and cried out: 'I'd rather be shot!' He struggled up from the hard ground.

All this made the broken-legged soldier very depressed. He gaped, his mouth half open, as if he had only just realised how serious things were. He had only spoken up to try and get in his brother's good books. He went and talked to the fellow again, but couldn't get any definite answer. So he tried to avoid the young man's [his brother's] eyes, and took his anger lying down, hoping that the awful news would only be a false rumour. But one day after a meal the men were taken off to the parade ground under the escort of a big group of armed soldiers.

When the officer read out the appalling order, his brother appealed against it. He was punished at once. He was given a dozen blows with a carrying pole, used in place of the normal military cane, and was locked up with several other men. But the broken-legged soldier went through the induction procedures as his turn came in the line, though his face went white and his knees trembled.

He made his mark in the volunteers' register and swore an oath that he would not desert. Finally they tattooed blue insignia on his arm. He got a uniform and then he was a real soldier. That day he began his life as a soldier, and at the same time his life became bitter with humiliation. Twice when they were numbering off he could not get his number out; the third time he got the number wrong, and was given a cuff round the ear. They used a special method to train him to goose-step – a strap was tied to each of his legs, and a seasoned soldier went in front of him pulling at them in turn. He was always being made to march at the double as punishment. He had never known tiredness before, but now as soon as he touched his bunk he fell asleep.

His brother was locked up for two months. He was supposed to be released one Sunday. The broken-legged soldier kept ticking the days off on his fingers. He gave up his day off, and early in the morning went off with an anxious heart to wait for their reunion. Towards evening he saw someone coming out of the company commander's quarters, his head bowed down in misery, a uniform tucked under his arm, a grey army cap perched on the back of his head, walking straight towards the back of the temple compound. The broken-legged soldier wanted to call out to him, but instead he scratched his neck, sighed and walked after him.

They sat down on the steps of a courtyard. From there they could look down into the little court, crowded with wild flowers and bushes; the croaking of frogs came on and off from the jade-green pool. A long time passed in solemn silence, then the broken-legged soldier started to fiddle with the strings of his straw sandals. He stole a glance at his brother.

'You're out?', he asked timidly.

The young man did not reply, just laid his head on his forearms. After a while he said, as if talking to himself:

'What's to be done? Everywhere we turn we run into some poisonous fate.'

'I'm going to escape', the young man said suddenly, lifting his head.

'Please don't think like that.' The broken-legged soldier looked round the empty courtyard. 'Escape. It's easy to say it. In the last month a dozen or so men have deserted, but only two or three got right away. You haven't seen how the others were punished. They were beaten worse than someone who has stolen an ox.' He walked over and stood in front of his brother, and said to him imploringly: 'Don't think like that. Just put up with it.'

'Put up with it! How can I put up with it? You haven't got any children, your wife is dead . . .'

'Don't say that kind of thing. Don't you think I miss home? I've had a very rough time – if it was easy to escape . . . you haven't seen the kind of abuse I've had . . . it's been awful.'

'So why are you telling me to put up with it?'

'I telling you what to do? Fine, do whatever you like, I shan't bother.'

The doctor smiled coldly. 'You certainly don't bother now', he said viciously.

'Well, what do you want me to do?' An awful pang of bad conscience almost stifled him, but he cried out 'Shall I go with you? Tell me what to do. I know it's only because of me that you got dragged into all of this.'

Neither of them said anything. Some time passed, and then the broken-legged soldier said with a slight choking sound: 'All right, I'll go with you', and then he lowered his eyes like a criminal, and didn't make another sound.

From that day on the broken-legged soldier had no peace. In the next two weeks, his brother found two opportunities to speak to him in secret, to talk to him about ways of deserting. Normally he simply dared not meet his brother's eyes, he was afraid of them, as if they were forcing him to make a decision. And when the young man approached him, a shiver of fear ran through his whole body. He felt that the officers already knew his secret, and were spying on him all the time.

One day his brother walked over to him on the parade ground.

'Wait at the Temple of the God of Wealth.'

'All right', the broken-legged soldier replied.

'Go round the side of the stables . . .'

'The company commander is watching us!' His eyes were full of fear. He put off going for a long while, then went off to the meeting with his brother. As the doctor laid out his plans, the broken-legged soldier couldn't tell whether he was listening to what he was saying, or to the sound of his own pounding heartbeats, or to all the fearful sounds of the twilight. From start to finish he kept his eyes on the ground, one hand fiddling with his buttons, as if he was standing in front of an officer getting a lecture. But he kept on echoing what his brother said, as if from habit, until his brother realised that he was in a state of panic. Then his brother pressed him hard: 'Huh! Why don't you open your mouth? Are you scared?'

The broken-legged soldier only lowered his head yet further.

'Are you scared or not? Tell me! Who's going to eat you?'

'I'm scared!' The broken-legged soldier finally got it out with a trembling voice. 'We might get caught. It's better to put up with things. I know it's all my fault that you got caught up in this . . .'

The young man shot a glance at him. 'It's no wonder people say you're useless!' And he glared at him, and dashed straight out of the temple hall.

The broken-legged soldier stayed on alone in the darkness. He sat there for a while, then buried his head in his hands. He was worried about his own fate, and anxious for his brother. He knew that he had not got the courage to desert, but he still did not dare to approach his brother. For from that night on, the young man was very cold towards him, and he always felt ashamed; if he ran into his brother, he unconsciously lowered his eyes, like a criminal. Whenever he thought of his brother's temperament, it made him shiver – whatever he said he would do he did. A month went by, and although there were one or two fewer comrades, his brother was there every day training on the sand flats. Now he was only worried about the officers' blows and curses.

It was one Saturday. The weather was fine and after breakfast all the soldiers went down to the river to wash their clothes. The weather was seldom good, and the officers had been accusing them of stinking for some time. The broken-legged soldier washed his uniform, then spread it out on the sand, and weighted it down with stones. Then he wrapped his arms round his shoulders and slipped into the trees beside the beach. Just when he had sat down on a rock, his brother came over to him, bare to the waist. This was the first time he had come up to him of his own accord for a month. He sat down beside him.

They sat in silence for a while, then the broken-legged soldier fixed his eyes on the tip of his straw sandals and timidly started to speak.

'You will have to settle down now' – he glanced at the doctor with his head down – 'I've heard that any deserters who are caught are going to be killed.'

'Isn't living this beggar's life here just the same? If we don't die of hunger we'll just be cannon fodder.'

The broken-legged soldier was beside himself. He opened his mouth wide but he could not get out a single sound.

The young doctor tossed away the pebbles he had been holding, stood up, and repeated: 'I've decided to escape.'

'What are you doing?'

'What? Why should I go on suffering here? You shouldn't write your funeral speech before you die [i.e. give up hope].'

The broken-legged soldier got up too, and said imploringly:

'Please listen to me.' But suddenly an officer came running over towards the trees, and their conversation was broken off.

The broken-legged soldier's feelings were in turmoil. He made up his mind to go on trying to persuade his brother [not to do it]. He had to be cautious, and everywhere he felt the eyes of spies, so he could not find a chance to talk to him. He could not sleep well at night; his ghastly fantasies would not let him sleep peacefully. He thought of his home, and his father. His wife, stretched out rigid on the bed, still seemed just the same as when he had gone into town. It seemed to him that his brother had already been caught trying to escape, that he had been tied up in the place where they usually beat deserters, and that the officers were holding lighted red joss-sticks in their hands. After a while he saw him lying on the sand of the execution ground, a thin dog standing beside his body. 'I did all this to him', he thought, and started to weep.

As he was hurrying to roll-call the next morning, almost all the soldiers were already assembled in their ranks, so he blinked his tired eyes, and slipped into the ranks, afraid of a beating or a cursing. The atmosphere was calm; he didn't hear any yelling. He just looked straight in front of him, at attention. The officers were discussing something earnestly, their voices low. One of them motioned towards him with his chin. The company commander called him out of the ranks. He told him that his brother had escaped in the night with two other men. He must know something about the details of the case.

At first the broken-legged soldier was so terrified that he could not get out a word; after a long while he hung his head and said: 'I ... I don't know.'

'Liar! You two brothers don't know what each other is doing? You were talking to each other under the trees yesterday when you were washing your clothes.'

'He didn't tell me anything. I ... I don't know anything about it.'

'You know about eating, don't you?' They gave him a few kicks and then locked him up in the detention hall.

He was locked up for five days, right to the time when two of the deserters who had been recaptured were released. As he came out of the small dark room, he suddenly recognised his brother at the door of a tent. There were blood-stains on the back of the young man's head; he was leaning against the door, his eyes fixed on the ground. He stood rooted to the spot for a while; his head seemed empty, like a football. He rubbed his neck, and didn't know what to do. Only when the soldiers who had come to release the deserters shouted at him did he come to his senses. He staggered over to his barrack.

Two or three of his room mates had already eaten their lunch. When they saw the hopeless look in his eyes, they stopped talking and looked at him. They asked him if he'd seen his brother. Had he worked out what to do for him? He sat silently on his bunk, covered his face with his hands, and started to moan softly.

'You're not a child. You must think of something to do.'

The broken-legged soldier poured out his anguish as if he were talking to himself. 'They're bound to kill him.'

'Are you going to go and plead for him?'

'My father would want me to stand in for him!'.

None of them could stop themselves from shaking their heads, and sighing; they all fell silent.

The broken-legged soldier got up, and wiped his eyes with the backs of his hands. 'I'm going to go and look for the company commander', he cried out, 'they can shoot me if they like.' He jumped up from his bed.

Without waiting, and without calling out his name, he went into the company commander's quarters. The officers were just in the middle of working out ways to punish the deserters, thinking of how to make an example of them. As soon as they saw him, they all flew into a rage. He stood mutely in front of them, trembling, one hand pulling at his trousers.

In the end, the duty officer with the red sash banged his fist on the table and shouted:

'What do you want? Is this the door of the mess?'

'I ... want ... I want to ask you a favour.'

'Fuck your favour. Get out!'

They hustled him out.

That afternoon they summoned him and made him shoot his brother with his own hand. Only after they had beaten him and cursed him for a long while could he carry out his orders. When he took aim the butt of the rifle slipped on his shoulder, just as he started to howl:

'He's my brother...'

Three times in a row he could not aim, so in the end two officers held him under the armpits and forced him to fire.

'GOOD AND EVIL EFFECTS OF WAR IN WEST CHINA'

The chronic insecurity and uncertainty of life under the domination of uncontrolled soldiers gave people very little control over the direction of their own lives. For most people the lack of control had negative implications, for some chaos meant opportunities, as these two stories from Archibald Adams, a missionary in Sichuan, attest. They were published in the *Chinese Recorder* for 1925, 408–9.

At the beginning of the year a young secretary of our Yachow [Yazhou] Young Men's Institute, a social service organisation of the Church, resigned his position because shortage of funds from America made it impossible for the Mission to raise his salary. Tempted by the high pay offered him to become a secretary to a military officer, he joined the army. Soon thereafter fighting began and his general was defeated, while he himself had several narrow escapes from death. Fleeing with the army to Kiating [Jiating] the young man came to see his old friends of the church and attended a conference retreat which was held by the Rev. K. T. Chung, General Secretary of the National Christian Council. Whether under the influence of these meetings or because of his narrow escapes from death, the young man decided to leave the army.

After writing a pathetic letter to one of the missionaries, he called and was advised to return to Yachow and apply for his old position or some other in the church he had deserted. Armed with a letter from the missionary he did this. The organisation he had deserted would not take him back but he was given a chance to prove that his repentance is genuine by being appointed to an outstation chapel as an evangelist.

The evil effects of the present civil war upon the innocent people are terrible. Let the following genuine incident illustrate this. Just now the battlefront is near the city of Mei Chou [Meizhou], half way between Kiating and Chengtu [Chengdu]. When the enemy was being driven out of the city by the north gate they first looted the shops and homes in the north suburb, and then set fire to the buildings. Among the helpless sufferers were two women – a widow and her daughter of eighteen. The soldiers first carried away her small store of rice and her pig, and then set her house on fire. She fled with her daughter walking where she could and getting a lift in passing boats, and finally arrived in Kiating where she had a nephew in charge of a boat she partly owned. To her dismay she found her boat commandeered to make the pontoon bridge and her nephew dead, his body awaiting burial. He had been seized by the military and forced to carry their loads for them but had escaped and was making his way back when the soldiers caught him and stabbed him in the side with a bayonet. Wounded and bleeding so as to be unable to walk he crawled twenty li (7 miles) all the way to Kiating, only to drop dead on reaching the ferry across from the city. The widow, his aunt, empty handed, had no means to bury him, but on telling her story to the boatmen and teashop keepers who knew her she was given enough money to bury the lad by them and is now making her home in the boat in the pontoon bridge. One of the teashop keepers is a member of our church. He came to me in great indignation and grief to tell me of this and other instances of the horror of this senseless and wicked civil war. His own business is so dead that he does not even open his shop, yet has to pay a heavy tax levied by the soldiers in support of the war. It is heart-hardening to have to sit by and see the misery of the people and yet be so helpless to assist them.

APPENDIX 8

'THE WORDS OF A SOLDIER'

This kind of revolutionary tract is rare. Except for the Guomindang armies on the Northern Expedition, and the Red Army, few Chinese units were actively involved in politics. We can assume from the date that this document had no immediate effect other than to get the person who wrote it and those who read it into serious trouble. What we can also see is the beginning of a consciousness that soldiers were nothing more than the pawns of their officers, playing in a dirty game in which all the rewards went to the officers and none to the soldiers. The consciousness is naive and impractical, and hardly likely to lead anywhere except a brief mutiny, but it is there nonetheless. This translation is taken from *Beiyang junfa tongzhi shiqi de bingbian*, pp. 263–7.

> Document apprehended by the Beiyang authorities,
> August 1920.

Brothers! I am a soldier of the 1st Company, 1st Battalion, 12th Regiment, 3rd Division. My name is Li Desheng, I come from Baoding in Zhili, and I have been in the army six or seven years; I have been in battle two or three times. Last year I was wounded in the leg by a shell during the fighting at Hengshan, and now, although my leg has recovered enough to let me walk, I still have not got the same freedom of movement as before. Two months ago I reported back to the battalion from sick leave, and was assigned to the guard house. Although I find the cries of my brothers being beaten when they are up on a charge hard to take, there is no drill, there are no real duties, and it's a quiet life. But every Sunday the people who visit their friends go off, and the people who go to the tea-house go off, and I am left on my own, because my leg bothers me and I don't like to drag up and down in front of other people. So I often sit in the guard room and talk to myself. Most of my old friends are dead, and the

new soldiers, seeing that I am disabled, have no particular interest in
me. Human relations are fleeting anyhow, so you can't blame them
for that. I might think of going home, but it's too far; I might think of
messing around outside for a while, but I don't think there's
anything to be said for that. It's just as difficult to go forward as back.
I feel gloomy every day, and I'm worried all the time. It is worse at
night, when it's even quieter, and I have great difficulty falling
asleep. I toss and turn, I think about the past and the future, but if I
concentrate on the present, I can't even look for my mother's affec-
tion any more. I don't make any predictions about whether I'll have
anything to eat in my old age or not. The things that you can't resolve
end up making the heart feel sour. One morning when I got up with a
worried frown stuck to my face, and was sunk deep in my troubles, a
friend gave me a book on which was written 'The words of a soldier'.
As soon as I saw the title I felt very peculiar. I opened the book, and
then read it from beginning to end several times. I felt that everything that I had wanted before I no longer wanted, that everything I
had lacked before I no longer lacked, that everything I had worried
about before I no longer worried about. I think that this book has had
an even greater influence on me than the Four Books and Five
Classics of Confucius and co. It really is a treasure beyond price,
and I have to tell my brothers this, to let them know this: the people
we killed before were all our brothers; the people we served before
were all our enemies, and they oppressed us; what we ate and what
we wore all came from the sweat of the common people, it wasn't the
marshal or the provincial warlords or the generals who paid out
money to support us. Brothers, I beg you to think this thing through
from top to bottom. Don't make our enemies into benefactors, and
blindly let them go on making fools of us. If you don't believe me,
wait until I have read 'The words of a soldier' aloud to you, sentence
by sentence:

Brothers, when we went into the army to be soldiers, was it for love of our
country, or was it to make a living? I believe we all went in to make a living;
no one would say it was for love of the country. What does that mean?
Brothers, just think, we all have families, but if you start to talk about
'country', which piece of land belongs to us poor people? Which particular
event has anything to do with us poor people? The people who are marshals
or high officers can run the areas under their control, they can levy taxes on
the people under their rule, they can requisition grain and other supplies.

They can also take the name of 'country', or of a province, and then take the things which ordinary people produce to make a living and pawn them or sell them to foreigners, get together some money and have a wild time with the young gentlemen, the young ladies and the older ladies [i.e. their families]. They use the country as their money tree, as their amulet; they use the people of the country as their slaves, as their chickens, their dogs, their cows or their horses. If they don't use the word 'country' then they cannot sell the products that the people make, or seize the people's food and clothing, so they are always patriotic with their mouths open, patriotic with their mouths shut. But we brothers, unless we are eating at home and don't have to spend any money, wherever we go outside, whoever we see, we always have to pay when we eat, and we have to pay for our clothes. Where is our 'country'? If we were not in the army, we would still have our families, but in the army we haven't even got our own family. And if as soldiers we go into battle, we may not even have our lives any more. Once when I went up to the front I saw lots of dead bodies lying around haphazardly by the roadside. There was no one to bury them. The bodies were covered in blood from head to foot; the stench was terrible. When I looked at their insignia I saw that they were all our brothers. I used to think that when soldiers died in battle it was a glorious and magnificent death, but when I saw that they had lost their arms or legs, that their brains had been dashed out or their stomachs had burst open, then the courage and the daring that our officers usually manage to plant in our stomachs faded away. Not only did it fade away, but I felt that all the training we had received in the regiment had oppressed us and duped us. Our bodies were born of our parents and we were raised by them; we were given a lot of kindness by our families, and we should love them. The country is another thing – what does it have to offer us? It can't be seen, it can't be heard, it doesn't respond to our calls. It is nothing but a few rogues who want to bully and oppress us, and to dupe us, and are afraid that we may see that it [the country] is only one individual, or one family, which we should not believe in. They create a country out of thin air, and raise it to a great height; they say that it has the right of life or death over people, and that people have the duty to serve it. Unless things are like this, they claim, there can be no peace on earth, and the people will have no one to protect them. The laws, the orders, the obedience, the rewards, the re-sistance, the violations, the beatings, the executions – all these pretexts are their private creations; they get us brothers to help them in the guise of the Chinese character 'country'. With these pretexts they can oppress us, kill us and even get us to kill their opponents. Without these pretexts, they would not be able to order people about, would not be able to be officers and make money. For this reason they are terrified of people who say they are wrong, and of books which say they are wrong. They hate them passionately and say they are disturbing the public order; if they don't confiscate the books then they arrest the people who criticise them. They call the books which oppose them prohibited books. They call the people who oppose them trouble-makers or revolutionaries or extremists. They put out general alerts to arrest the opponents and seize the prohibited books. We brothers have not realised that the people and the books who oppose them are all defending the ordinary people against injustice, and have many interests in common with us. Instead we obey their orders and confiscate the books and arrest the people; we gather all the good people and all the good books into one net, and let a few evil things ride rough-shod over us all. Please tell me if we can, in conscience, justify this or not? Think, comrades! First of all we have no property, secondly we have no status, thirdly we are barely literate. What do these oppositionists and prohibited books have to do with us? A marshal gets several million yuan a year; a provincial warlord gets several hundred thousand; a division commander gets eight hundred ounces of silver a month, not including the expenses of his office. A brigade commander gets four hundred ounces, a regimental commander three hundred, a battalion commander two hundred and the company commander fifty. The platoon commander gets twenty-four, the quartermaster twenty. But people like us, the junior privates, make at most 4.8 ounces, and the senior privates 5.2. When you deduct living expenses from these four or five ounces, there isn't enough left for pocket money, so how can we talk of sending money to our families? Even though the revolutionaries want to turn the world upside down, surely it can't be said that you and I will have nothing to eat? The revolution is aimed against officers and officials, against the upper classes, the rich; it is not aimed against the ordinary people, nor does it plan to kill our fathers and mothers, rape our wives, steal our possessions. How can we treat the revolutionaries as enemies? If the revolution is successful, not only will we never have to worry about food and clothing again, but we will be able to live out our days in peace and unity. Everyone on earth, no matter who they are, will be our equals then, quite different from now. Is that good or not? Now these people who are officials and merchants put on airs all the time, keeping up their face. Not only do they not till the land or weave cotton; they do not even understand how these things are done. So what do they rely on for food and clothing? They have created something to deceive people, and called it 'money'. The merchants take money and exchange it for food and clothes. They buy cheaply and sell expensively, and make a profit out of the deals. The people who are officials find that in collecting taxes, it is much more convenient to demand money than to demand grain, so they welcome the money that the merchants scatter around. With the passage of time money has become something that can do anything. Look at the people who have money – don't they buy presidents, don't they buy members of parliament, don't they buy us soldiers to die for them? The people who sell their votes for the presidency, the members of parliament who sell their votes get at most several hundred thousand yuan each, at least several hundred. People like us who are soldiers get four or five ounces of silver a month when we are alive. When we are dead we get no more than fourteen dollars and twenty cents – ten dollars for the coffin, four for a shroud, and a few cents for paper [various accoutrements of the funeral]. If they put it kindly, they say we died in the firing line; if they put it nastily, they say we deserted in the face of the enemy. Is this injustice or not? The people who are officials depend either on taxes for their livelihood or on borrowing money from abroad. If they don't maintain soldiers then they cannot impose taxes, nor is anyone willing to help them borrow money from foreigners. So they take the vile money they have grabbed from the common people, and they take the money they have got from selling the masses' goods to the foreigners. What they give to us soldiers is less than a drop in the ocean. They order the officers to keep us under strict control, and get us to oppress the ordinary people – even our own parents, our relatives and our friends. Usually they are extremely harsh to us. If they raise their hands it is to strike us, if they open their mouths it is to curse us. If there is a little dispute, they say we are resisting our officers; the severest punishment is execution, the lightest a flogging. In general they train us to kill our flesh and blood, to take our bodies and our guns and to follow orders and march. When it comes to using us in battle, they do not stint on money for rice, and give us biscuits to eat, like people in prison who only get a full meal just before the guns are raised to shoot them. Some comrades who don't realise that they have not got a shred of good will towards us still welcome battle, and look forward to being promoted to officers and making money. In fact in every unit there are always plenty of people waiting to fill the places of officers, but don't forget that in the army regulations, soldiers are always soldiers, and officers are always officers, and it is very difficult to break a rule and let someone leap up from being a soldier to being an officer. Out of a thousand men, not one will succeed. As for making money, that is an empty dream. When you brothers are at the front, they tell you that you can do well. But the canteens which follow the units are viciously expensive, and since no one knows when they are going to meet their end, everyone likes to eat and drink. If you have a few dollars in your hand, you either eat it up or drink it up, and what you hang on to is very little. Brothers, if you joined up to make money, I dare say that you are dreaming. If you joined up to get food to eat and clothes to wear, I dare say that you actually have got food to eat and clothes to wear, and not only do you have them, but your wives and children do too. But what of all these things were not made by us poor people? If we make them, we should consume them too. Brothers! From now on we must not obey our officers' orders, we must not use our guns to kill the ordinary people, to kill our brothers. We must use our guns to help the workers and the peasants to make revolution against the officials and the financiers and the merchants. We must force them to return all the things which were seized from us or taken by deceit; we must teach them not to puff themselves up, to die of overeating while other people die of starvation, to die of warmth while others die of cold, to die of sweetness while others die of bitterness, to die of leisure while others die of overwork. We are all human beings, all born on a piece of earth. Isn't it better for us all to live peacefully and equitably? Why do we need to scramble for power and profit? Why do we need to get fat off the backs of others? Recently in Germany and Austria things became so inequitable and so unjust that the ordinary people rose in rebellion, and shook heaven and earth, even more ferociously than in Russia. Our Chinese workers there were strongly in support of them. It was really the will of heaven. Brothers, if we are willing to act as watchdogs for these financiers for four or five ounces of silver, to act as their executioners, then there is nothing for me to say, except that I expect you to shed some tears when you kill me. But if you think that they are individuals, and we are too, and we are not willing to act as watchdogs for them, to be their executioners, then we must all make up our minds to chase away our own officers, and link up with the peasants and the workers, take all the things that are left behind and use them ourselves, but take the money that things were sold for and tell them to take it. Anything that can be eaten or worn or lived in or used can be left for anyone to eat or wear or live in or use. When this gets under way, things will be chaotic for a while, but when the chaos is over, everything will be fine. It is like what happens when you rearrange the furniture and decorations of a big house which has a lot of people living in it: first you have to get rid of all the people, and all the furniture and decorations. While you are doing that, isn't there chaos in the house? Or when soldiers are on parade, and the lines change from horizontal to vertical, or from two lines to four lines or eight lines; first there is chaos and then the new lines are formed. The good that comes from chaos is no different. Brothers! Be courageous and do it. If the common people's revolution is begun by us soldiers, if we take this great cause and spread it to the masses, I don't think there will be any opposition to us. For the fates of all men, and the weapons are in our hands. Don't worry that someone is an official, or a financier. They have no power except to trick the people. What are we afraid of? There are four principles we must give:

1. The land which produces the five grains and cotton and all valuable things should be publicly owned. Anyone can use it. It should not be privately owned by landlords.
2. All food and clothing and lodging should be exchanged for labour. Anyone who can work should work.
3. All things are produced from the strength of men of the past and of the present, and they should be enjoyed by everybody.
4. Men should be equal to men, women equal to women, women to men, men to women. No one should cheat others, or take rents or act as officials. All matters should be settled by discussion.

This book was written to persuade my brothers. It is too simplistic. It was set down by a certain brother from the 2nd Route.

I have now finished reading 'The words of a soldier'. My brothers who suffer with me, isn't what he says true? The time has come. Let us rise up swiftly, and get rid of these things which oppress us.

When you have read this, please pass it on. Those who can read please read it aloud to those who cannot.

NOTES

ABBREVIATIONS

CWR – China Weekly Review
CYB – China Year Book
NCH – North China Herald

INTRODUCTION

1. For a good discussion of the military's role in the 1911 Revolution, see Edmund Fung, *The Military Dimension of the Chinese Revolution.*
2. Ch'i Hsi-sheng, *Warlord Politics in China*, p. 79.
3. Chen Zhirang (Jerome Ch'en), *Junshen zhengquan*, p. 83.
4. *NCH*, 24 February 1923, 497.
5. Geliefu, *Zhongguo jundui zhi yanjiu*, p. 22.
6. Martin Van Krefeld, *Supplying War*, p. 110.
7. Lu Pingdeng, *Sichuan nongcun jingji*, p. 362.
8. Philip Kuhn, *Rebellion and its Enemies in Late Imperial China*, p. 14.
9. Alfred Vagts, *The History of Militarism*, p. 14.
10. Feng Hefa, *Zhongguo nongcun jingji lun*, p. 362.
11. Feng Hefa, *Zhongguo nongcun jingji ziliao (xubian)*, p. 644.
12. Zhang Youyi (ed.), *Zhongguo jindai nongye shi ziliao*, III (1927–37), pp. 636 ff; and Xiao Meng, 'Shandong Zhaoyuan xian nongcun gaikuang', in Qian Jiaju (ed.), *Zhongguo nongcun jingji lunwen ji*, p. 556. See also Chen Zhengmo, *Gesheng nonggong guyong xiguan ji xuhong zhuangkuang*, p. 66.
13. Thomas Gottschang has recently shown a very high degree of localisation in migration from Shandong and Hebei to Manchuria. See his 'Migration from North China to Manchuria: an economic history, 1881–1942', unpublished Ph.D. thesis, University of Michigan, 1982. I thank Thomas Rawski for this reference.
14. Diana Lary, 'Warlord studies', *Modern China*, VI, 4 (October 1980).
15. Examples of some of the more recent studies of specific categories of people are: Delia Davin, *Women/Work*, Oxford, 1976; Roxanne Witke and Margery Wolf, *Women in Chinese Society*, Palo Alto, 1975; and Steven Andors, *Workers and Work Places*, New York, 1976.

16. A wide variety of military journals exists to satisfy the vicarious interest in violence. Some of the more respectable are: *Combat Ready*; *Mercenary*; *Soldiers of Fortune*; *Warrior*; and my favourite, *Diana Armi*.
17. Lary, 'Warlord studies'.
18. Tao Menghe, 'Yige jundui bingshi de diaocha', *Shehui kexue zazhi*, 1, 2 (June 1930).
19. David Hackett Fischer, *Historians' Fallacies*, p. 90.
20. *Ibid.*, p. 94.
21. Albert Feuerwerker, *Economic Trends in the Republic of China*, p. 16.

1. SOURCES OF SOLDIERS

1. Zhongyang lujun junguan xuexiao, *Xinbing jingshen jiaoyu wenda*, p. 5.
2. Victor Kiernan, 'Conscription and society in Europe before the War of 1914 to 1918', in M. R. D. Foot (ed.), *War and Society*, p. 148.
3. Zhu Zhixin, *Zhu Zhixin ji*, p. 368.
4. *NCH*, 3 June 1916, 530.
5. Joseph Esherick, *Reform and Revolution in China*, pp. 143–50.
6. Liu Ruming, *Liu Ruming huiyi lu*, pp. 2–3.
7. Donald Jordan, *The Northern Expedition*, pp. 232–8.
8. Lei Haizong, *Zhongguo wenhua yu Zhongguo de bing*, gives a general description of conscription in Chinese history. The specific quotation is from Jun Heng, 'Jianshe you bing wenhua', *Duli pinglun*, 27 September 1936, 2–3.
9. Liu Gongren, *Zhongguo lidai zhengbing zhidu*, pp. 115–17.
10. Tao Xisheng, *Zhongguo shehui zhi shi de fenxi*, p. 129.
11. Diana Lary, *Region and Nation*, pp. 183–5.
12. *NCH*, 5 December 1914, 714.
13. Lary, *Region and Nation*, pp. 170–82.
14. Geliefu, *Zhongguo jundui zhi yanjiu*, p. 21.
15. Li Jiren, 'Bing dabo Chen Zhenwu de yuepu', *Dongfang zazhi*, XXIV, 4 (24 February 1927), 87.
16. Robert Kapp, *Szechwan and the Chinese Republic*, p. 60.
17. Liu Xiaosang, *Zhongguo guomin bingyi shilue*, p. 90.
18. Evans Carlson, *The Chinese Army*, p. 31.
19. *Henansheng 1937 xianyi shiling zhuangding tongji biao*, 124/267, 16745, Dier lishi danganguan, Nanjing.
20. Zi Qi, 'Zhengbing xinzheng xia de Subei nongcun', *Zhongguo nongcun*, July 1937, 69.
21. Shen Congwen, *Xiangxi*, p. 27.
22. Lin Zhenpu, *Bingyi zhi gailun*, pp. 240–3.
23. John Service, *Lost Chance in China*, p. 11.
24. Zhao Fu, 'Geming jun de jinxi guan', *Geming pinglun*, XII, July 1928, 52–3.

25. Mao Wei, 'Sannian lai Dongbei yijun', *Dongfang zazhi*, XXXII, 6 (16 March 1935), 58.
26. *NCH*, 21 July 1923, 162.
27. Zhongguo renmin zhengfu xieshang huiyi chuanguo weiyuanhui, *Xinhai geming huiyi lu*, Beijing, 1961, v, p. 504.
28. *Xinbing jingshen jiaoyu*, p. 1
29. Tao Menghe, 'Yige jundui bingshi', 99.
30. *NCH*, 14 October 1917, 78.
31. *Xuanwei xianzhi gao* (1934), 455–7.
32. Geliefu, *Zhongguo jundui*, p. 20.
33. Zhang Youyi (ed.), *Zhongguo jindai nongye*, II, p. 69.
34. Luo Ertian, *Junfa yiwen*, p. 234.
35. Liu Ruming, *Liu Ruming huiyi lu*, p. 1.
36. Luo Ertian, *Junfa yiwen*, p. 77.
37. Cai Tingkai, *Cai Tingkai zizhuan*, pp. 53–4.
38. Zhongguo wenti yanjiu zhongxin, *Peng Dehuai*, p. 5.
39. Jiang Baili, 'Caibing jihua shu', in *Jiang Baili xiansheng chuanji*, IV.
40. Xi Chao, 'Henan nongcun zhong de pianyue laodong', *Dongfang zazhi*, XXXI, 18 (16 September 1934), 71.
41. Geliefu, *Zhongguo jundui*, p. 18.
42. Lary, *Region and Nation*, p. 25.
43. Wu Shoupeng, 'Douliu yu nongcun jingji shidai de Xuhai geshu', *Dongfang zazhi*, XXVII, 6 (16 March 1930), 70–2.
44. *Shuyang xiangtu zhi*, p. 71.
45. Lu Feng, *Gangtie de duiwu*, p. 4.
46. *Linquan xianzhi lu* (1936), 12.
47. Sha Ting, 'Ji He Long', in *Hongqi piaopiao*, VI, p. 107.
48. *NCH*, 10 July 1910, 1.
49. Tao Xisheng, *Chaoliu yu diandi*, pp. 155–6.
50. *Xinhai geming huiyi lu*, VI, pp. 518, 520.
51. Li Zongren, 'Li Zongren huiyi lu', *Mingbao*, CXLIX (May 1978), 92.
52. Chen Hansheng, *Guangdong nongcun shengchan guanxi yu shengchan li*, p. 65.
53. *Ibid.*
54. Tao Xisheng, *Chaoliu yu diandi*, p. 16. A list of specific transfers is cited in Chen Zhirang, *Junshen zhengquan*, p. 75.
55. For other instances of long-distance recruitment, see Wen Gongzhi, *Zuijin sanshinian Zhongguo junshi shi*, II, pp. 234, 271; *NCH*, 27 July 1918, 199, 28 September 1918, 739; *CWR*, 7 April, 1923, 214, 12 July 1924, 196.
56. Liu Ruming, *Liu Ruming huiyi lu*, p. 21.
57. Shen Congwen, *Biancheng*, pp. 8–9.
58. *Ibid.*
59. Li Tsung-jen and Tong Te-kong, *The Memoirs of Li Tsung-jen*, pp. 4–5.
60. Chen Zhengmo, *Gesheng nonggong*, p. 61.

61. The first quotation is from L. Arlington, *Through the Dragon's Eye*, the second from Henry Misselwitz, *The Dragon Stirs*, p. 14.

2. GOING INTO THE ARMY

1. Feng Yuxiang, *Wode dushu shenghuo*, pp. 27–9.
2. *CYB* (1924–5), 911.
3. Ralph Powell, *The Rise of Chinese Military Power*, p. 10; and Kuhn, *Rebellion and its Enemies*, pp. 147–8.
4. Zhang Qiyun, 'Lidai zhi bingyuan yu jiangcai', *Sixiang yu shidai*, XVI, 17 (1942), 117.
5. Liu Ruming, *Liu Ruming huiyi lu*, p. 28.
6. *Ibid.*, p. 36.
7. Cai Tingkai, *Cai Tingkai zizhuan*, pp. 171, 185.
8. Shijiu lujun congjiehuibu jiaodaodui, *Tongxue lu*, no pagination.
9. *NCH*, 11 August 1917, 317.
10. Liu Ruming, *Liu Ruming huiyi lu*, p. 28.
11. *CWR*, 16 February 1924, 44; and Wen Gongzhi, *Zuijin sanshinian*, II, p. 333.
12. Donald Sutton, *Provincial Militarism and the Chinese Republic*, p. 273; and Liu Jianqun, 'Wo yu Long Yun', *Zhuanji wenxue*, I, 6 (November 1962), 17.
13. Li Jiren, 'Bing dabo', *Dongfang zazhi*, XXIV, 3 (10 February 1927), 92–3.
14. Henry Misselwitz, 'The Chinese soldier, his employment and activities', *CWR*, 7 July 1928, 191.
15. *Xuanwei xianzhi gao*, 455–7.
16. Zhang Youyi (ed.), *Zhongguo jindai nongye*, II, p. 69.
17. *Linqu xuzhi* (1935), 44.
18. Wang Renshu, *Xiangzhang xiansheng*, p. 20.
19. While in flight, in 1930, Shi Yousan 'ordered' 1,000 recruits in Guangcong (Hebei) – but could not stay long enough to collect them. *Guangcong xianzhi* (1934), I, p. 17 (2).
20. Liu Ruming, *Liu Ruming huiyi lu*, p. 28.
21. Geliefu, *Zhongguo jundui*, p. 20.
22. *Linqu xuzhi*, 44.
23. Feng Yuxiang, *Wode shenghuo*, pp. 181–2.
24. Zhang Youyi (ed.), *Zhongguo jindai nongye*, II, p. 649.
25. Tsen Shi-yu, 'We must abolish our system of mercenary troops', *CWR*, 12 June 1926, 34–5.
26. *Yunnan gailan, junshi*, p. 1.
27. Feng Yuxiang, *Wode shenghuo*, p. 182.
28. Liu Fenghan, *Xinjian lujun*, p. 98; and Fung, *The Military Dimension*, p. 73.
29. A. R. Skelley, *The Victorian Army at Home*, p. 237.

30. *CYB* (1916), 296.
31. Feng Yuxiang, *Wode shenghuo*, pp. 181–2.
32. Shen Congwen, *Congwen zizhuan*, pp. 60–3.
33. *Xinhai geming huiyi lu*, v, p. 504.
34. Shen Yanbing, *Zhongguo de yiri*, ii, p. 6.
35. Liu Fenghan, *Xinjian lujun*, p. 98.
36. *CYB* (1916), 296.
37. Feng Yuxiang, *Wode shenghuo*, p. 182.
38. *NCH*, 18 August 1923, 458.
39. Chen Guofu, *Xiao yisi ji*, p. 323.
40. *Xinhai geming huiyi lu*, i, pp. 49, 68.
41. Gavan MacCormack, *Chang Tso-lin in Northeast China*, p. 104.
42. Shen Congwen, *Congwen zizhuan*, pp. 76, 84–5.
43. Fung, *The Military Dimension*, part i.
44. Wang Ermin, *Huaijun zhi*, pp. 126–7.
45. Tao Zhuyin, *Beiyang junfa tongzhi shiqi shihua*, i, pp. 5–6.
46. Zhu Zhixin, *Zhu Zhixin ji*, ii, p. 373.
47. Wen Gongzhi, *Zuijin sanshinian*, ii, p. 249.
48. *Ibid.*, p. 278.
49. William Whitson, *The Chinese High Command*, p. 10.
50. James Sheridan, *Chinese Warlord*, p. 160.
51. *Xin Hankou*, i, 11 (May 1930), 95.
52. Wen Gongzhi, *Zuijin sanshinian*, ii, p. 156.
53. Charles Finney, *The Old China Hands*, pp. 70–1.
54. Fei Rong, 'Junren keju xia de Sichuan nongmin', *Xin zhuangcao*, ii, 1–2 (1932), 184; and Lu Pingdeng, *Sichuan nongcun*, jingji p. 362.
55. Liu Yimin, 'Fujian de mintuan yu nongcun', *Xin zhuangcao*, ii, 1–2 (July 1932), 245.
56. Wang Ermin, *Huaijun zhi*, p. 118.
57. Jerome Ch'en, *The Military/Gentry Coalition*, p. 82.
58. *Guangcong xianzhi*, vi.
59. Liu Yimin, 'Fujian de mintuan', 248.
60. Mao Zedong, *Mao Zedong xuanji*, i, p. 41.
61. Wen Gongzhi, *Zuijin sanshinian*, ii, p. 347.
62. Otto Braun, *Chinesische Aufzeichnungen*, p. 23.
63. Samuel Griffith, *The Chinese People's Liberation Army*, p. 30.

3. LIFE IN THE ARMY

1. A. A. Milne, *The World of Christopher Robin*, London, 1958, p. 8.
2. Maurice Janowicz, *Sociology and the Military Establishment*, p. 44.
3. Geliefu, *Zhongguo jundui*, p. 24.
4. Wufu, 'Ruwu shenghuo', *Shiri tan*, xxxvii (20 August 1934), 96.
5. Geliefu, *Zhongguo jundui*, p. 66.

6. Li Zongren, 'Li Zongren huiyi lu', *Mingbao*, CXLIX (May 1978), 92.
7. Jian Youwen, *Xibei dongnan feng*, p. 17; Liu Ruming, *Liu Ruming huiyi lu*, p. 4; and *NCH*, 1 March 1924, 322.
8. Guomin geming zhengfu junshi weiyuanhui, *Gemingjun lianzuofa*, p. 3.
9. Guomin geming zhengfu junshi weiyuanhui, *Xinbing duben*, p. 2.
10. *Shibing zhoukan*, LXX (January 1948), 16.
11. Wufu, 'Ruwu shenghuo', 96.
12. Tao Menghe, 'Yige jundui bingshi', 95–6.
13. Shijiu lujun congjiehuibu jiaodaodui, *Tongxue lu*, no pagination.
14. Janowicz, *Sociology*, p. 48.
15. Zhu Zhixin, *Zhu Zhixin ji*, II, p. 377.
16. *NCH*, 26 May 1953, 211.
17. *Chinese Recorder* (July 1913), 456.
18. John Hall, *The Yunnanese Provincial Faction, 1927–1937*, p. 42.
19. Feng Yuxiang, *Wode dushu shenghuo*, p. 10.
20. Wen Gongzhi, *Zuijin sanshinian*, II, p. 258.
21. Wang Shunu, *Zhongguo changzhi shi*, p. 329.
22. For a longer discussion, see chapter 6.
23. *NCH*, 8 July 1922, 87.
24. Florence Nightingale, 1863.
25. Li Tsung-jen and Tong Te-kong, *Memoirs of Li Tsung-jen*, p. 48.
26. *NCH*, 24 July 1922, 200.
27. Figures for 1915 are from *CYB* (1916), 298; 1926 Guangzhou figures are from *CWR*, 27 March 1926, 99; 1926 Guangxi figures are from Li Zongren, 'Li Zongren huiyi lu', *Mingbao*, CXLVIII (April 1978), 82; and 1929 Taiyuan figures are from Tao Menghe, 'Yige jundui bingshi', 118.
28. Lary, *Region and Nation*, p. 44.
29. Jian Youwen, *Xibei dongnan feng*, p. 13.
30. *NCH*, 20 July 1918, 144.
31. John Chang, 'Mutiny cases in China since the Revolution', *CWR*, 24 February 1923, 501–4.
32. *NCH*, 3 July 1915, 20.
33. Cai Tingkai, *Cai Tingkai zizhuan*, p. 137.
34. Li Zongren, 'Li Zongren huiyi lu', *Mingbao*, CXLVIII (April 1978), 83.
35. Shen Congwen, *Congwen zizhuan*, p. 68.
36. Cai Tingkai, *Cai Tingkai zizhuan*, p. 89.
37. *Ibid.*, p. 66.
38. Li Ji, 'Bing dabo', *Dongfang zazhi*, XXIV, 4 (24 February 1927), 93.
39. Cai Tingkai, *Cai Tingkai zizhuan*, p. 116.
40. Li Zongren, 'Li Zongren huiyi lu', *Mingbao*, CXLIV (December 1977), 100.
41. Shen Congwen, *Congwen zizhuan*, p. 117.
42. *Dongfang zazhi*, III, 6 (June 1904), 99.
43. *NCH*, 6 January 1923, 10.

44. Shen Yanbing, *Zhongguo de yiri*, IV, p. 7.
45. Geliefu, *Zhongguo jundui*, p. 21.
46. Tao Menghe, 'Yige jundui bingshi', 105.
47. *Ibid.*, 103.
48. *Ibid.*, 105.
49. Shen Congwen, *Congwen zizhuan*, p. 3.
50. Cai Tingkai, *Cai Tingkai zizhuan*, pp. 103, 137.
51. *CYB* (1916), 296.
52. Liu Ruming, *Liu Ruming huiyi lu*, p. 38.
53. *NCH*, 13 October 1923, 89.
54. Tanaka Tadao, *Guoming geming yu nongmin wenti* (trans. Li Youwen), p. 232.
55. Shi Fen, 'Luo Binghui jiangjun shengping' in *Hongqi piaopiao*, V, p. 187.
56. Liu Ruming, *Liu Ruming huiyi lu*, p. 5.
57. Shen Congwen, 'Jianshe', in *Shen Congwen xuanji*, pp. 137–40.
58. Shen Congwen, *Congwen zizhuan*, p. 63.
59. Peng Yuting, 'Lun mintuan yu jundui', in Kong Xiexiong, *Zhongguo jinri nongcun yundong*, p. 215.

4. OFFICERS AND MEN

1. Gwynn Harries-Jones, *The Army in Victorian Society*, p. 3.
2. Luo Ergang, 'Qingji bingwei jiangyou de qiyuan', *Zhongguo shehui jingji shi jikan*, V, 2 (1937).
3. Geliefu, *Zhongguo jundui*, pp. 18–20.
4. Kapp, *Szechwan*, p. 38.
5. Sheridan, *Chinese Warlord*, p. 84.
6. Liu Ruming, *Liu Ruming huiyi lu*, p. 14.
7. Cai Tingkai, *Cai Tingkai zizhuan*, p. 140.
8. Sutton, *Provincial Militarism*, p. 277; and Fung, *The Military Dimension*, p. 25.
9. Lary, *Region and Nation*, pp. 35–8.
10. Morton Fried, 'Military status in Chinese society', *American Journal of Sociology*, LVII (January 1952), 347–57.
11. Liu Fenghan, *Xinjian lujun*, p. 109.
12. Geliefu, *Zhongguo jundui*, p. 28.
13. Li Zongren, 'Li Zongren huiyi lu', *Mingbao*, CXLV (January 1978), 102.
14. Ouyang Ju, *Guangzhoushi lujun zaixiang junguan huiyuan mingce*. Figures cited from this source are inexact because the volume is very tightly bound and parts are therefore illegible.
15. Li Liguo, 'Wanbei suweiai de chuangshiren zhi yi Wei Yanzhou', *Hongqi piaopiao*, V, p. 23.
16. *CYB* (1929–30), 750.
17. Li Zongren, 'Li Zongren huiyi lu', *Mingbao*, CXLIX (May 1978), 89.

18. Guangdongsheng junguangqu, *Junxun jiangyi*, pp. 86–94.
19. Shen Congwen, *Congwen zizhuan*, p. 58.
20. Zhongyang lujun junguan xuexiao, *Xinbing jingshen jiaoyu wenda*, p. 9.
21. Xiao Jun, 'Jun zhong', in *Yang*, pp. 111–42.
22. Wufu, 'Ruwu shenghuo', *Shiri tan*, XXXVIII (20 August 1934), 96.
23. Feng Yuxiang, *Wode shenghuo*, p. 187.
24. *Ibid.*, p. 188.
25. *NCH*, 23 September 1922, 869.
26. Li Tsung-jen and Tong Te-kong, *Memoirs of Li Tsung-jen*, pp. 80–1.
27. Dixon, N., *On the Psychology of Military Incompetence*, pp. 173–93.
28. Li Zhupi, *Jundui weisheng xue*, p. 1.
29. *CWR*, 11 October 1924, 194.
30. Hunansheng zhengfu tongji shi, *Xiangzheng liunian tongji, junwu*, no pagination.
31. Li Zhupi, *Jundui weisheng*, p. 85.
32. Feng Yuxiang, *Wode shenghuo*, p. 184.
33. Feng Changjiang, *Zhongguo de xibei jiao*, p. 27.
34. Evans Carlson, *The Chinese Army*, pp. 51–4.
35. Munroe Scott, *McClure: The China Years*, pp. 117–18.
36. For accounts of the maltreatment of conscripts, see Jack Belden, *China Shakes the World*, and Theodore White and Annalee Jacoby, *Thunder out of China*.
37. Service, *Lost Chance*, p. 114.

5. BANDIT/SOLDIER — SOLDIER/BANDIT

1. Lary, *Region and Nation*, pp. 43–5.
2. *NCH*, 9 June 1923, 658.
3. Wu Zhixin, 'Zhongguo nongmin licun wenti', *Dongfang zazhi*, XXXIV, 15 (10 September 1937), 18.
4. Kong Xuexiong, *Zhongguo jinri de nongcun yundong*, p. 183.
5. *Lingxian xuzhi* (1936), 463 ff.
6. *Chaocheng xian xuzhi* (1920), 241.
7. He Xiya, *Zhongguo daofei wenti zhi yanjiu*, p. 45.
8. Anthony Chan, *Arming the Chinese*. The book deals with the arms trade and industry in warlord China.
9. Duanmu Xiazhen, 'Shuyang xian nongcun gaikuang', *Shenbao yuekan*, IV, 12 (December 1935), 73.
10. *NCH*, 2 December 1922, 578.
11. *CWR*, 12 January 1924, 248.
12. *CWR*, 30 March 1930, 164.
13. Feng Hefa, *Zhongguo nongcun jingji ziliao*, p. 492.
14. Yan Zhongda, 'Hubei xibei de nongcun', *Dongfang zazhi*, XXIV, 16 (24 August 1927), 44.

15. *NCH*, 20 March 1912, 163.
16. *NCH*, 17 August 1918, 388.
17. Eric Teichman, *Travels of a Consular Officer in North-West China*, pp. 74–5.
18. Wen Gongzhi, *Zuijin sanshinian*, II, p. 99.
19. *NCH*, 22 September 1923, 827.
20. *NCH*, 10 February 1923, 363.
21. Cen Chunxuan, *Lezhai manbi*, pp. 11–2.
22. MacCormack, *Chang Tso-lin*, p. 17.
23. Lary, *Region and Nation*, p. 24.
24. *Linqu xuzhi* (1935), 44.
25. *NCH*, 1 September 1915, 11.
26. Huang Shaoxiong, *Wushi huiyi*, p. 36; and Wen Gongzhi, *Zuijin sanshinian*, II, p. 336.
27. *NCH*, 10 February 1912, 369.
28. *NCH*, 18 August 1918, 328.
29. Tan Shi-hua, with S. Tretiakov, *Chinese Testament*, p. 175.
30. *NCH*, 6 April 1918, 328.
31. *CWR*, 2 June 1923, 3.
32. *CWR*, 21 July 1923, 246.
33. *CWR*, 16 June 1923, 80.
34. Huang Shaoxiong, *Wushi huiyi*, pp. 64–5.
35. *CWR*, 29 December 1923, 181.
36. *CWR*, 10 November 1923, 466; and 26 January 1924, 310.
37. He Yixian, 'Zou Maping shoubian', in *Xinghuo liaoyuan*, I (xia), p. 662.
38. *Hexian zhi* (1934), 212.
39. Harvey Howard, *Ten Weeks with Chinese Bandits*, pp. 115–16.

6. GREY RATS AND GREY WOLVES

1. Quoted in Liu Jingan, 'Henan minge zhong de feizai yu bingzai', *Minsu*, CX (30 April 1930).
2. Kong Xuexiong, *Zhongguo jinri de nongcun yundong*, p. 186.
3. Li Tsung-jen and Tong Te-kong, *Memoirs of Li Tsung-jen*, pp. 112–13.
4. Li Zongren, 'Li Zongren huiyi lu', *Mingbao* CXLIII (November 1977), 23.
5. For a more detailed study of army depredations, see Ch'en *The Military/Gentry Coalition*. See also Sheridan, *Chinese Warlord*; Donald Gillin, *Warlord: Yen Hsi-shan in Shansi Province*; and Kapp, *Szechwan*.
6. Tao Dingguo, 'Nongcun zhong bingchai wenti zhi jiantao', *Nongcun jingji*, II, 7 (May 1935); and Wang Yansheng, *Zhongguo beibu de bingchai yu nongmin*.
7. Fei Rong, 'Junren keju xia de Sichuan nongmin', *Xin zhuangcao*, II, 1–2 (22 July 1932); and Wang Yansheng, *Zhongguo beibu*.
8. Feng Hefa, 'Binchai yu nongmin', *Zhongguo nongcun jingji lun*, p. 355; and Tao Dingguo, 'Nongcun zhong bingchai', p. 4.

9. *NCH*, 5 December 1917, 307.
10. *Qufu xianzhi* (1934), v, 11–12.
11. Li Jinghan, *Dingxian shehui gaikuang diaocha*, p. 775.
12. *NCH*, 12 February 1924, 501.
13. Teichman, *Travels of a Consular Officer*, p. 64.
14. Lary, *Region and Nation*, pp. 46–7.
15. *NCH*, 6 December 1919, 620.
16. Li Tsung-jen and Tong Te-kong, *Memoirs of Li Tsung-jen*, pp. 69–70.
17. T'ien Chün, *Village in August*, pp. 105–7.
18. *NCH*, 12 January 1923, 10.
19. *NCH*, 9 January 1923, 598.
20. *NCH*, 19 May 1923, 435.
21. *NCH*, 21 April 1923, 156.
22. *NCH*, 5 March 1924, 171.
23. Li Jinghan, *Dingxian shehui*, p. 781.
24. *NCH*, 13 October 1923, 98.
25. Zhu Zhixin, *Zhu Zhixin ji*, ii, p. 381.
26. *NCH*, 17 January 1920, 141.
27. *NCH*, 9 August 1919, 359.
28. Elly Widler, *Six Months Prisoner of the Szechwan Military*, p. 65.
29. Li Jiren, 'Bing dabo', *Dongfang zazhi*, xxiv, 4 (24 February 1927), 80.
30. Graham Greene, *Lawless Roads*, p. 120.
31. P. Bardis, 'Violence: theory and quantification', *Journal of Political and Military Sociology*, i, 1 (1973), 127.
32. *Dali xianzhi gao* (1916), 435–5.
33. *CWR*, 10 May 1924, 398.
34. Lary, *Region and Nation*, p. 53.
35. Sha Ting, 'Tubing', in *Fuzi de gushi*.
36. Li Zongren, 'Li Zongren huiyi lu', *Mingbao*, cxliv (December 1977), 100.
37. Kapp, *Szechwan*, p. 53.
38. Feng Hefa, 'Bingchai yu nongmin', p. 389.
39. Lu Teng (trans.), 'Huabei nongcun shehui yinluo ji', *Zhongguo laodong*, i (October 1935), 93.
40. Sha Ting, 'Ji He Long', *Hongqi piaopiao*, vi, p. 108.
41. Feng Hefa, 'Bingchai yu nongmin', p. 387.

7. BAD IRON

1. I. H., 'Wuhua yundong', *Nuli zhoubao*, 17 September 1922, 3.
2. Widler, *Six Months Prisoner*, p. 66.
3. Lawrence Impey, 'Chinese progress in the art of war', *CWR*, 27 December 1924, 103.
4. Widler, *Six Months Prisoner*, p. 109.

5. Huang Zhuyi, 'Chuanbei nongmin xiankuang zhi yiban', *Dongfang zazhi*, xxiv, 16 (24 August 1927), 38.
6. Skelley, *The Victorian Army at Home*, p. 245.
7. Luo Ertian, *Junfa yiwen*, p. 51; and *NCH*, 19 November 1923, 371.
8. Zhou Wen, 'Didi', in *Fuzi zhi jian*, pp. 1–19.
9. Chang Kuo-t'ao, *The Rise of the Chinese Communist Party*, pp. 10–11:
10. Feng Yuxiang, *Feng Yuxiang xunling*, pp. 14, 15, 52.
11. Guomin geming zhengfu junshi weiyuanhui, *Gemingjun lian zuofa*, p. 4.
12. *Shibing zhoukan*, LXX (January 1948), p. 16.
13. *NCH*, 7 April 1923, 18.
14. Zhu Zhixin, *Zhu Zhixin ji*, II, p. 433.
15. *Ibid.*, pp. 462–3.
16. Jaroslav Hašek, *The Good Soldier Švejk* (trans. Cecil Parrott), p. 76.
17. Feng Hefa, *Zhongguo nongcun jingji ziliao (xubian)*, p. 355.
18. Shen Congwen, *Congwen zizhuan*, pp. 68–9, p. 74.
19. Zhu Zhixin, *Zhu Zhixin ji*, II, p. 375.
20. Bernd Martin, *Die Deutsche Beraterschaft in China, 1927–1928*, p. 385, 390.
21. Interview with 'Mad Mike' Hoare, C.B.C. 'Sunday Morning', 6 December 1981.

8: LEAVING THE ARMY

1. Cai Tingkai, *Cai Tingkai zizhuan*, pp. 69, 72.
2. Sha Ting, 'Xiongshou', in *Sha Ting xuanji*, pp. 91–100.
3. *CYB*, 1924–5, 954.
4. Li Tsung-jen and Tong Te-kong, *Memoirs of Li Tsung-jen*, p. 260.
5. *Junshi weiyuanhui gongbao*, II (10 August 1928), 75.
6. *Ibid.*, xvii (10 October 1928), 96.
7. *Ibid.*, xvii (10 October 1928), 96.
8. Liu Fenghan, *Xinjian lujun*, p. 101.
9. Li Jiren, 'Bing dabo', *Dongfang zazhi*, xxiv, 3 (10 February 1927), 96.
10. J. Keegan, *The Face of Battle*, pp. 113, 181–2, 241.
11. Cai Tingkai, *Cai Tingkai zizhuan*, p. 116.
12. W. Whitson, *The Chinese High Command*, p. 13.
13. Lary, *Region and Nation*, p. 74.
14. *Junshi weiyuanhui gongbao*, xvii, 62.
15. *CWR*, 1 March 1924, 24.
16. He Huiyuan, 'Lun junfei', *Duli pinglun*, 15 July 1934, 15.
17. Sheridan, *Chinese Warlord*, p. 152; and Institute of Pacific Research, *Agrarian China*, p. 49.
18. He Xiya, 'Jiazi dazhan hou chuanguo jundui zhi diaocha', *Dongfang zazhi*, xxii, 1 (10 January 1925), 103.
19. Zong Yan, 'Caibing jihua de taolun', *Dongfang zazhi*, xix, 14 (24 July 1922), 139.

20. *NCH*, 25 November 1922, 503.
21. Li Zongren, 'Li Zongren huiyi lu', *Mingbao*, CLVI (December 1978), 66.
22. Chen Zuiyun, 'Fuxing nongcun zhengce', *Geming pinglun*, 28 March 1937, 37.
23. Lary, *Region and Nation*, p. 134.
24. Li Tsung-jen and Tong Te-kong, *Memoirs of Li Tsung-jen*, p. 260. The situation in the Chinese armies was less gross than that in Spain. In 1921, the Spanish Army had 20,000 officers for 200,000 men; there were 690 generals, and 2,000 colonels. No officer once commissioned could be persuaded to resign. Edward Feit, *The Armed Bureaucrats*, p. 24.
25. *NCH*, 14 February 1914, 429; and Zhang Xing, *Fujian daofei gaikuang yu suiqing quyi*, p. 12.
26. Zong Yan, 'Caibing jihua', 20.
27. *NCH*, 9 September 1914, 903.
28. *Chinese Recorder* (1922), 742.
29. *CWR*, 25 October 1924, 256.
30. *NCH*, 10 June 1916, 567.
31. Zhu Zhixin, *Zhu Zhixin ji*, II, pp. 373–4.
32. *Shibing zhoukan*, LXIII (1947), no pagination.
33. Fan Changjiang, *Zhongguo de xibei jiao*, p. 11.

9. MILITARISM AND CHRONIC VIOLENCE

1. John Gunn, *Violence in Human Society*, p. 28.
2. *Ibid.*, p. 43.
3. Franco Fornari, *The Psychoanalysis of War*, pp. 5–6.
4. Elizabeth Perry, *Rebels and Revolutionaries in North China*.
5. Judith Stacey, *Patriarchy and Socialist Revolution in China*, p. 967.
6. Sidney Gamble, *Peking: A Social Survey*, p. 409.
7. Yen Ching-yueh, 'Crime in relation to social change in China', *American Journal of Sociology*, XL, 3 (1934), 302.
8. *Ibid.*, 298.
9. Samuel Huntington, *Political Order in Changing Societies*, p. 200.
10. Maury Feld, *The Structure of Violence: Armed Forces as Social Systems*, p. 20. For a study of the arms trade from the West to China, see Anthony Chan, *Arming the Chinese*.
11. Claude Welch and Arthur Smith, *Military Role and Rule*, p. 58.
12. Eric Nordlinger, *Soldiers in Politics: Military Coups and Governments*, p. 2.
13. Katherine Chorley, *Armies and the Art of Revolution*, p. 242.
14. Ch'en, *The Military/Gentry Coalition*.
15. W. J. M. Mackenzie, *Power, Violence, Decision*, p. 145.
16. Lionel Tiger, *Men in Groups*, p. 175.
17. *NCH*, 2 October 1933, 362.
18. Li Zongren, 'Li Zongren huiyilu', *Mingbao*, CXLIV (December 1977), 101.

19. Fan Changjiang, *Zhongguo de xibei jiao*, p. 39.
20. *CWR*, 12 February 1924, 202.
21. *Ping Han nianjian* (1932), pp. 640–1.

BIBLIOGRAPHY

CHINESE SOURCES

Cai Tingkai. *Cai Tingkai zizhuan*. Hong Kong, 1946.

Cen Chunxuan. *Lezhai manbi*. Beiping, 1943.

Chaocheng xianzhi xuzhi. 1920.

Chen Gengguang. 'Zhongguo nongcun shenchan yu shehui xianzhuang', *Zhongguo laodong daxue yuekan*, 1, 3 (March 1930).

Chen Guofu. *Xiao yisi ji*. Nanjing, 1947.

Chen Hansheng. *Guangdong nongcun shengchan guanxi yu shengchan li*. Shanghai, 1934.

Chen Zhengmo. *Gesheng nonggong guyong xiguan ji xuhong zhuangkuang*. Nanjing, 1935.

Chen Zhirang. *Junshen zhengquan*. Hong Kong, 1979.

Dali xianzhi. 1937.

Dongfang zazhi. Shanghai, 1904–48.

Duanmu Xiazhen. 'Shuyang xian nongcun gaikuang', *Shenbao yuekan*, IV, 12 (December 1935).

Duli pinglun. Beiping, 1927–37.

Fan Changjiang, *Zhongguo de xibei jiao*. Tianjin, 1936.

Fei Rong. 'Junren kezhu xia de Sichuan nongmin', *Xin zhuangcao*, II, 1–2 (22 July 1932).

Feng Hefa. *Zhongguo nongcun jingji lun*. Shanghai, 1934.

Zhongguo nongcun jingji ziliao. Shanghai, 1935.

Feng Yuxiang. *Wode dushu shenghuo*. Shanghai, 1947.

Wode shenghuo. N.p., 1947.

Xunling. Shanghai, n.d.

Gao Jing. 'Women zenmeyang gaicao tufei?', in *Kangjan zhong de Zhongguo nongcun yuntai*. N.p., 1939.

Geliefu. *Zhongguo jundui zhi yanjiu* (trans. Wei Yimin). N.p., 1933.

Guangcong xianzhi. 1933.

Guomin geming zhengfu junshi weiyuanhui. *Gemingjun lian zuofa*. Nanjing, 1928.

Xinbing duben. N.p., n.d.

Junshi weiyuanhui gongbao. Nanjing, 1928–38.

Junshi zazhi. Nanjing, 1928–38.

Hankoushi zhengfu. *Xin Hankou*. Hankou, 1929–31.
He Xiya. *Zhongguo daofei wenti zhi de yanjiu*. Shanghai, 1925.
Hexian zhi. 1934.
He Yixian. 'Zou Maping shoubian', in *Xinghuo liaoyuan*, I, xia.
Henansheng 1937 xianyi shiling zhuangding tongji biao. Zhongguo dierlishi
     danganguan, 124/267 16745.
Huang Shaoxiong. *Wushi huiyi*. Hangzhou, 1945.
Hunansheng zhengfu tongji shi. *Xiangzheng liunian tongji*. Changsha,
     1942.
Jian Youwen. *Xibei dongnan feng*, Shanghai, 1935.
Jiang Baili. *Jiang Baili xiansheng chuanji*. Taibei, 1971.
Kong Xuexiong. *Zhongguo jinri de nongcun yundong*. Shanghai, 1934.
Lei Haizong. *Zhongguo wenhua yu Zhongguo de bing*. Changsha, 1940.
Li Dongfang. *Zhongguo zhanshi de yanjiu*. Chongqing, 1934.
Linquan xianzhi lu. 1936.
Linqu xuzhi. 1935.
Lingxian xuzhi. 1936.
Li Jinghan. *Dingxian shehui gaikuang diaocha*. Beiping, 1933.
Li Nanli and Wu Rui. *Yige putong zhanshi de changchang – Liu Zilin de gushi*.
     Beijing, 1954.
Li Zhupi. *Jundui weisheng xue*. Changsha, 1939.
Li Zongren, 'Li Zongren huiyi lu', *Mingbao*, CXXXVI–CLVI (1977–8).
Lin Zhenpu. *Bingyi zhi gailun*. N.p., 1940.
Liu Fenghan. *Xinjian lujun*. Taibei, 1967.
Liu Gongren. *Zhongguo lidai zhengbing zhidu*. Chongqing, 1941.
Liu Jianqun 'Wo yu Long Yun', *Zhuanji wenxue*, I, 6 (November 1962).
Liu Jingan. 'Henan minge zhong de feizai yu bingzai', *Minsu*, CX (April
     1930).
Liu Ruming. *Liu Ruming huiyi lu*. Taibei, 1966.
Liu Xiaosang. *Zhongguo guomin bingyi shilue*. N.p., 1940.
Liu Yimin. 'Fujian de mintuan yu nongcun', *Xin zhuangcao*, II, 1–2 (July
     1932).
Lu Deng. 'Huabei nongcun shehui yinluo ji', *Zhongguo laodong*, I (October
     1935).
Lu Feng. *Gangtie de duiwu*. Hong Kong, 1947.
Lu Pingdeng. *Sichuan nongcun jingji*. Shanghai, 1936.
Luo Ergang. 'Qingji bingwei jiangyou de qiyuan', *Zhongguo shehui jingji shi
     jikan*, V, 2 (1937).
Luo Ertian. *Junfa yiwen*. Taibei, 1972.
Mao Zedong. *Mao Zedong xuanji*, I. Beijing, 1964.
Ouyang Ju. *Guangzhoushi lujun zaixiang junguan huiyuan mingce*. Guangzhou,
     1948.
Pan Guangdan. 'Shuo jun yu min', *Zhengxue zui yan*. Shanghai, 1948.
Peng Shuzhi. 'Women de Beifa guan', in *Lun Beifa*. N.p., 1926.

Peng Yuting. 'Lun mintuan yu jundui', in Kong Xiexiong, *Zhongguo jinri nongcun yundong*. Shanghai, 1934.

Ping Han tielu guanli weiyuanhui, *Ping Han nianjian*. Hankou, 1932.

Qian Jiaju (ed.). *Zhongguo nongcun jingji lunwen ji*. Shanghai, 1936.

Sha Ting. 'Ji He Long', *Hongqi piaopiao*, VI.

'Tubing', in *Fuzi de gushi*. Shanghai, 1963.

'Xiongshou', in *Sha Ting xuanji*. Hong Kong, 1956.

Shen Congwen. *Biancheng*. Shanghai, 1948.

Congwen zizhuan. Hong Kong, 1960.

Ruwu hou. N.p., 1928.

Shen Congwen xuanji. Shanghai, 1931.

Xiangxi. N.p., 1944.

Shen Yanbing. *Zhongguo de yiri*. Shanghai, 1936.

Shibing zhoukan. Beiping, 1947–8.

Shijiu lujun congjiehuibu jiaodaodui. *Tongxue lu*. N.p., 1933.

Shuyang xiangtu zhi, Taibei, 1974.

Tanaka Tadao. *Guoming geming yu nongmin wenti* (trans. Li Youwen). Beiping, 1930.

Tao Dingguo. 'Nongcun zhong bingchai wenti zhi jiantao', *Nongcun jingji*, II, 7 (May 1935).

Tao Menghe. 'Yige jundui bingshi de diaocha', *Shehui kexue zazhi*, I, 2 (June 1930).

Tao Xisheng. *Chaoliu yu diandi*. Taibei, 1963.

Zhongguo shehui zhi shi de fenxi. Shanghai, 1929.

Tao Zhuyin. *Beiyang junfa tongzhi shiqi shihua*. Beijing, 1957.

Tian Wen. 'Guibing yu nong jihua', *Geming pinglun*, XIII (July 1928).

Wang Ermin. *Huaijun zhi*. Taibei, 1967.

Wang Renshu. *Xiangzhang xiansheng*. Shanghai, 1936.

Wang Shunu. *Zhongguo changzhi shi*. Shanghai, 1935.

Wang Yansheng. *Zhongguo beibu bingchai yu nongmin*. Shanghai, 1931.

Wen Gongzhi. *Zuijin sanshinian Zhongguo junshi shi*. Shanghai, 1932.

Wufu. 'Ruwu shenghuo', *Shiri tan*, XXXVIII (20 August 1934).

Xiao Jun. 'Jun zhong', in *Yang*. Hong Kong, 1952.

Xie Bingyin. *Yige nubing de zizhuan*. Shanghai, 1936.

Xuanwei xianzhi gao. 1934.

Xuxiu Qufu Xianzhi. 1934.

Yunnan gailan, n.p., n.d.

Zhang Qiyun. 'Lidai zhi bingyuan yu jiangcai', *Sixiang yu shidai*, XVI, 17 (1942).

Zhang Xing. *Fujian daofei gaikuang yu suiqing quyi*. N.p., 1933.

Zhang Youyi (ed.). *Zhongguo jindai nongye shi ziliao*, II (1912–27) and III (1927–37). Beijing, 1957.

Zhang Zhongwu. *Shuyang xiangtu zhi lue*. Taibei, 1974.

Zhao Fu. 'Geming jun de jinxi guan', *Geming pinglun*, XII (July 1928).

Bibliography

Zhongguo dier lishi danganguan. *Beiyang junfa tongzhi shiqi de bingbian.* Nanjing, 1984.

Zhongguo nongcun jingji yanjiu hui. *Zhongguo nongcun.* Guilin, 1934–43.

Zhongguo qingnian chuban she. *Hongqi piaopiao.* Beijing, 1957–61.

Zhongguo renmin jiefangjun ershinian zhengwen bianji weiyuanhui. *Xinghuo liaoyuan.* Beijing, 1960.

Zhongguo renmin zhengfu xieshang huiyi chuanguo weiyuanhui. *Xinhai geming huiyi lu.* Beijing, 1961.

Zhongguo wenti yanjiu zhongxin. *Peng Dehuai.* Hong Kong, 1969.

Zhongyang lujun junguan xuexiao. *Xinbing jingshen jiaoyu wenda.* Chongqing, n.d.

Zhou Wen. 'Didi', in *Fuzi zhi jian.* Shanghai, 1934.

Zhou Zhizhang. 'Zhongguo nongcun zhong de bingchai', *Xin zhuangcao,* II, 1–2 (July 1932).

Zhu Zhixin. *Zhu Zhixin ji.* Shanghai, 1921.

I. H. 'Wuhua yundong', *Nuli zhoubao,* September 1922.

WESTERN LANGUAGE SOURCES

Arlington, L. *Through the Dragon's Eye.* London, 1931.

Bardis, P. 'Violence: theory and quantification', *Journal of Political and Military Sociology,* I, 1 (1973).

Belden, J. *China Shakes the World.* New York, 1970.

Billingsley, P. 'Bandits, baresticks and bosses', *Modern China,* VII, 3 (July 1981).

'Some notes on banditry', *Chinese Republican Studies Newsletter,* VI, 1 (October 1980).

Braun, O. *Chinesische Aufzeichnungen.* Berlin, 1973.

Carlson, E. F. *The Chinese Army.* New York, 1940.

Chan, Anthony. *Arming the Chinese.* Vancouver, 1983.

Chang Kuo-t'ao. *The Rise of the Chinese Communist Party.* Lawrence, Kansas, 1971–2.

Ch'en, J. *The Military–Gentry Coalition.* Toronto, 1979.

Ch'i Hsi-sheng. *Warlord Politics in China.* Stanford, 1976.

China Weekly Review. Shanghai (1917–50).

China Year Book. Tientsin and Shanghai (1912–39).

Chinese Recorder. Shanghai (1896–1941).

Chorley, K. *Armies and the Art of Revolution.* London, 1943.

Dixon, N. *On the Psychology of Military Incompetence.* London, 1975.

Esherick, J. *Reform and Revolution in China.* Berkeley, 1976.

Feit, E. *The Armed Bureaucrats.* Boston, 1973.

Feld, M. *The Structure of Violence: Armed Forces as Social Systems.* Beverly Hills, 1977.

Feuerwerker, A. *Economic Trends in the Republic of China.* Ann Arbor, 1977.

Finney, C. J. *The Old China Hands*. New York, 1963.

Fischer, D. H. *Historians' Fallacies*. New York, 1970.

Foot, M. R. D. (ed.). *War and Society*. London, 1973.

Fornari, F. *The Psychoanalysis of War*. New York, 1974.

Fried, M. 'Military status in Chinese society', *American Journal of Sociology*, LVII (January 1952).

Fung, E. *The Military Dimension of the Chinese Revolution*. Vancouver, 1980.

Gamble, S. *Peking: A Social Survey*. Peking, 1921.

Gillin, D. *Warlord: Yen Hsi-shan in Shansi Province*. Princeton, 1967.

Griffith, S. *The Chinese People's Liberation Army*. New York, 1967.

Greene, G. *Lawless Roads*. London, 1939.

Gunn, J. *Violence in Human Society*. Newton Abbot, 1973.

Gutteridge, W. *Military Institutions and Power in the New States*. London, 1965.

Hall, J. C. S. *The Yunnanese Provincial Faction, 1927–1937*. Canberra, 1976.

Harries-Jones, G. *The Army in Victorian Society*. London, 1977.

Hatano Yoshihiro. 'The New Armies', in Mary Wright (ed.), *China in Revolution*. New Haven, 1968.

Harvard University, Committee on International and Regional Studies. *Biographies of Kuomintang Leaders*. Cambridge (Mass.), 1948.

Hašek, J. *The Good Soldier Švejk* (Schweik). Translated by Cecil Parrott. London, 1973.

Howard, H. *Ten Weeks with Chinese Bandits*. London, 1927.

Howard, M. *War in European Society*. London, 1976.

Hsiao Kung-ch'uan. *Rural China: Imperial Control in the Nineteenth Century*. Seattle, 1960.

Huntington, S. *Political Order in Changing Societies*. New Haven, 1968.

Impey, L. *The Chinese Army as a Military Force*. Tientsin, 1926.

Institute of Pacific Research. *Agrarian China*. Shanghai, 1938.

Janowièz, M. *Military Institutions and Coercion in the Developing Nations*. New York, 1977.

   Sociology and the Military Establishment. New York, 1959.

Jordan, D. *The Northern Expedition*. Hawaii, 1976.

Kapp, R. *Szechwan and the Chinese Republic*. New Haven, 1973.

Keegan, J. *The Face of Battle*. London, 1974.

Kuhn, P. *Rebellion and its Enemies in Late Imperial China*. Cambridge (Mass.), 1970.

Lary, D. *Region and Nation*. Cambridge, 1975.

   'Second Historical Archives, Nanjing', *Modern China*, VII, 4 (October 1981).

   'Warlord studies', *Modern China*, VI, 4 (October 1980).

Lee, J. 'Food supply and population growth in Southwest China, 1250–1850', *Journal of Asian Studies*, XLI, 4 (August 1982).

Li Tsung-jen and Tong Te-kong. *The Memoirs of Li Tsung-jen*. Boulder, 1979.

Liu, F. F. *A Military History of Modern China*. Princeton, 1956.

Bibliography

MacCormack, G. *Chang Tso-lin in Northeast China, 1911–1928*. Paolo Alto, 1977.

Mackenzie, W. J. M. *Power, Violence, Decision*. London, 1975.

Martin, B. *Die Deutsche Beraterschaft in China, 1927–1938*. Düsseldorf, 1981.

Misselwitz, H. *The Dragon Stirs*. Westport, 1941.

Naquin, S. *Millenarian Rebellion in China*. New Haven, 1976.

Nordlinger, E. *Soldiers in Politics: Military Coups and Governments*. Englewood Cliffs, 1977.

North China Herald. Shanghai (1910–41).

Perry, E. *Rebels and Revolutionaries in North China*. Palo Alto, 1980.

Powell, R. *The Rise of Chinese Military Power*. Princeton, 1955.

Scott, M. *McClure: The China Years*. Toronto, 1977.

Service, J. S. *Lost Chance in China*. New York, 1974.

Sheridan, J. *Chinese Warlord*. Palo Alto, 1966.

Skelley, A. R. *The Victorian Army at Home*. London, 1977.

Slawinski, R. *La société des piques rouges et le mouvement paysan en Chine en 1926–7*. Warsaw, 1975.

Spence, J. *The Death of Woman Wang*. London, 1978.

Stacey, J. *Patriarchy and Socialist Revolution in China*. Berkeley, 1983.

Sutton, D. *Provincial Militarism and the Chinese Republic*. Ann Arbor, 1980.

Tan Shih-hua, with S. Tretiakov. *Chinese Testament*. London, 1934.

Teichman, E. *Travels of a Consular Officer in North-West China*. Cambridge, 1921.

T'ien Chün. *Village in August*. London, 1942.

Tiger, Lionel. *Men in Groups*. New York, 1969.

Vagts, Alfred. *The History of Militarism*. New York, 1967.

Van Krefeld, M. *Supplying War*. Cambridge, 1977.

Welch, C. and Smith, A. *Military Role and Rule*. North Scituate, 1974.

White, T. and Jacoby, A. *Thunder out of China*. New York, 1946.

Whitson, W. *The Chinese High Command*. New York, 1973.

Widler, E. *Six Months Prisoner of the Szechwan Military*. Shanghai, n.d.

Yen Ching-yueh. 'Crime in relation to social change in China', *American Journal of Sociology*, XL, 3 (1934).

INDEX

174

military discipline, 36, 50
military elite, 5, 49
military schools, 51–2
military, scorn for, 22, 101
militia, Guangxi, 16
militiamen, 8
militias, 34, 61
missionaries
  and soldiers, 40, 58, 78, 81, 99
  reporting on soldiers, 73
mutinies, 43, 55, 74, 99

Napoleon Bonaparte, 43
neglect, of soldiers, 56–8
  callousness of officers, 58
  lack of health care, 56, 57
  lack of sanitation, 57
  poor living conditions, 56
New Armies, 1, 2, 8, 14, 29, 30, 31
Nightingale, Florence, 41
non-commissioned officers, 36, 37
non-military culture, 15
North China Herald, 10, 73
Northern Expedition, 14, 17, 38, 51, 58, 95, 97

officers, 49–58, 90
officer–men relations, 49–51, 58
  caste separation, 49
  contractual, 50, 58
  distinction of function, 49
  indifference and neglect, 50, 58
  predatory, 51, 58
'Onward Christian soldiers', 38
opium smoking, 29, 40, 86

pay, army, 18, 42–6, 51
pay, labourers', 46
Peng Dehuai, 19
Peng Yuting, 48
People's Liberation Army, 7, 86
Perry, Elizabeth, 103
Post Office, the Chinese, 45
Powell, J. P., 65
praetorian society, 104
predators, soldiers as, 23
press-ganging
  of coolies, 16, 60, 73–4
  of soldiers, 94
promotion, from ranks, 46, 52
prostitution, 40, 41, 86

Qi Xieyuan, 19
quarters, army, 56, 79

railways, 42
rape, 41, 76, 77, 81, 86
recruitment
  of armed men, 32, 62
  competitive, 28
  continuous process, 24, 35, 93
  as employment, 22
  ethnic minorities, 21
  family connections, 24, 36
  and labour surplus, 23
  through local government, 27
  of men of violence, 20–1
  of militiamen, 33
  personal ties in, 25, 26
  of scum of society, 29, 83, 85
  standards, 29–31
  street, 28–9
recruitment areas, 6, 19, 22
recruitment brokers, 27
Red Army, 15, 17, 34, 38, 49, 52, 66, 69, 78, 86
Red Spears, 81
regions of violence, 20
remittances, from soldiers, 45
retirement, of soldiers, 99, 100
Rockefeller, John D., 65
Russian Army, 41, 53

sadism, of officers, 56
sanbing, see scattered soldiers
scattered soldiers, 32, 33, 68, 77
Second Historical Archives (Nanjing), 11
secret societies, 20, 82
Sha Ting, 9, 81, 93
Shen Congwen, 22, 43, 44, 45, 54, 88
  'Construction' ('Jianshe'), 46–8
  education, 31
  enlistment, 30
  as soldier, 9
Shen Hongying, 59, 69
Smedley, Agnes, 73
Snow, Edgar, 73
soldiers, British, 13, 30, 41, 84–5
soldiers, Chinese
  age range, 39
  behavioural excesses, 39
  characteristics, 83–6
  class consciousness, 89, 105, 106
  'cultured', 15

Index